PUTTING
TRADITION
ON TRIAL

PUTTING TRADITION ON TRIAL

*Why the Resurrection of the Son of God
Did Not Occur on a Sunday (or Saturday)*

Patrick Cavanagh

Library of Congress Control Number:		2014911196
ISBN:	Hardcover	978-1-4931-9195-6
	Softcover	978-1-4931-9194-9
	eBook	978-1-4931-9196-3

Rev. date: 12/22/2014

To order additional copies of this book, contact:
Xlibris
0-800-443-678
www.Xlibris.co.nz
Orders@Xlibris.co.nz
511195

Introduction

As a result of recent advances in technology, many historical court judgements have been successfully challenged.

These challenges are often referred to as 'cold case' investigations, which has engendered widespread interest and even TV programmes based upon *fictional* cold cases.

Putting Tradition on Trial is a *factual* examination of one of the oldest cold cases on record—the death and resurrection of the Son of God almost 2,000 years ago—based upon the *literal* texts of the source documents as they appear in the ancient Hebrew and Greek manuscripts.

Throughout the ages, some of the written evidence related to this subject has been examined and re-examined by the best-qualified theological minds available, and yet their conclusions have historically differed greatly, as we can see from the various doctrines that have developed from them.

Yet the more this issue was studied, the more it became obvious that there are significant errors in current popular traditional doctrines that are based upon the Bible.

'The Trial' scrutinizes some of the popular versions upon which these doctrines are founded.

Anyone searching the Internet for guidance on this subject will be aware that we are now confronted with a bewildering range of theories to choose from.

For many believers, this has resulted in a lingering uncertainty about which version of events is true.

Because we will be contesting the documentary evidence upon which historical decisions relating to this subject are based, we must, as any good lawyer would advise, be conversant with 'the details in the fine print' recorded in those ancient documents.

In a court of law, ignorance of those details inevitably leads to a failure to prove one's case, as many have discovered to their consternation and cost. But surely misunderstanding a few biblical texts shouldn't make any meaningful difference to important Christian doctrines, should it?

This was the view of the respected theologian Sir Frederick Kenyon, who offered the following opinion:

> No fundamental doctrine of the Christian faith rests on a
> disputed reading. It cannot be too strongly asserted that in
> substance the text of the Bible is certain: especially is this
> the case with the New Testament.

Since the subject under investigation in 'The Trial' concerns one of the most fundamentally important doctrines of the Christian faith, the death and resurrection of the Son of God, the evidence about to be introduced will determine whether or not that claim is supported by fact.

Contrary to Sir Frederick Kenyon's statement, the apostle Paul warned that even in his day the evangel was already being distorted.

The Concordant Literal New Testament:

> I am marveling that thus, swiftly, you are transferred from that which calls you in the grace of Christ to a different evangel, which is not another, except it be that some who are disturbing you want also to distort the evangel of Christ. But if ever we also or a messenger out of heaven should be bringing you an evangel beside that which you accepted, let him be anathema. (Galatians 1:6-8).

This warning to the Galatians has particular relevance to the subject under scrutiny in 'The Trial' because whilst all studies on this subject obviously *do* promote the death and resurrection of the Son of God, many important details in the fine print have been distorted or omitted, resulting in Paul's words, 'a different evangel, which is not another'.

Although Sir Frederick Kenyon acknowledged that there were (and there still are) 'disputed readings', the inevitable conclusion to be drawn from the evidence submitted in 'The Trial' is that these disputed readings and the doctrines emanating from them have caused irreconcilable schisms between groups of sincere believers throughout the ages.

Paul also warned:

The Concordant Literal New Testament:

> Who hinders you not to be persuaded by the truth? This
> persuasion is not of Him Who is calling you. A little leaven
> is leavening the whole kneading' (Galatians 5:9).

Apparently, little had changed by the time of Jerome, who about 350
years later wrote: 'So great is the force of established usage that even
acknowledged corruptions please the greater part, for they prefer to
have their copies pretty rather than accurate.'

To pursue this study, some simple well-established facts and a *literal*
translation of the ancient Greek texts must be considered.

The literal translations of the Greek texts that appear throughout 'The
Trial' are from **the Concordant Literal New Testament (CLNT),
the Concordant Version of the Old Testament (CVOT),** and **the
Concordant Version of the Sacred Scriptures: Greek Text with
English Sublinear and Superlinear** (uncial) **(CLNTGT),** using
an eclectic selection of the appropriate texts from the ancient Greek
codices—**Sinaiticus, Alexandrinus, and Vaticanus.**

(Published by the Concordant Publishing Concern, 15570 West
Knochaven Road, Canyon Country, CA 91351, U.S.A.)

Where accents, parentheses, and abbreviations appear (in all
quotations) throughout 'The Trial', they were inserted by the author.

These will be compared with three commonly used representative versions: **The King James Version (KJV)**, Printed and published by William Collins, Sons and Company, Limited (1948); **the New American Standard Bible (NASB)** (reference edition, published by Foundation Press Publications, Box 277, La Habra, California, 90631 for the Lockman Foundation); and **the Revised Standard Version (RSV)** (published by Wm. Collins & Co. Ltd for the British and Foreign Bible Society in the format of the Bible Society's Third Jubilee Bible edited by John Stirling).

Everywhere, other than quotations from the above versions, where *God's name* appears in 'The Trial', it will be transliterated as **YHWH**,* from the four Hebrew letters it is composed of (the Tetragrammaton) throughout the Hebrew scriptures.

* The Concordant Version of the Old Testament contains '**Yahweh**' in most books of the Old Testament, which is a way it is commonly pronounced.

God's name, **YHWH**, appears 6,828 times in the Hebrew texts but in most bibles was replaced and now appears as '**Lord**'.

This arbitrary substitution is directly responsible for the adoption of unscriptural doctrines and is in contradiction of what **YHWH** has said about His name, which He intended to be known by all people.

CVOT: 'And you will say in that day: "Acclaim **Yahweh**! Proclaim His name!"' (Isaiah 12:4).

The text is absolutely clear. The name that will be proclaimed on that day will be **YHWH**, not **Lord** or any other hybrid version of it.

CVOT: 'Thus says my LORD **Yahweh**: "Behold! I shall lift up My hand to the nations and to the peoples I shall raise high My banner . . . Then you will know that I am **Yahweh**; those who are expectant in Me shall not be ashamed . . . Then all flesh will know that I **Yahweh** am your Saviour and your Redeemer' (Isaiah 49:22, 23, 26).

CLNT: 'For the Scripture is saying to Pharaoh that: "For this selfsame thing I rouse you up so that I should be displaying in you My power and so that My name should be published in the entire earth"' (Romans 9:17).

When **YHWH** was originally pronounced, it did not contain a 'J' (non-existent in the Hebrew language), which is now a substitution of the original 'Y' (*yohd*); neither did it contain a 'V', a substitution of 'W' in later times. Consequently, the renditions that contain those letters in a reformed version of the name are fundamentally inaccurate.

In spite of the frequency of the appearance of **YHWH**'s name throughout the Hebrew texts, it appears that only Orthodox Christianity cannot identify with certainty the (unchangeable) name of their God, the only true God (John 17:3), but use instead substitute names and titles.

No such liberty has ever been taken with the name of the adversary, Satan, which is pronounced in English almost as it has always been in Hebrew—apart from the accent, which in Hebrew usually falls on the last syllable, whereas in English it is invariably on the first.

In 'The Trial', the name of God's Son is written as it is pronounced—*Yaishua*—from the vowel-pointed Hebrew texts of the Old and New Testaments (e.g. Professor Franz Delitzsch's New Testament Hebrew translation).

The Masoretes, who were responsible for the vowel-pointing of the Hebrew texts, placed the vowel indicator for the vowel 'tsere' (two horizontal dots) between the first and second consonants yohd or 'y' and shin or 'sh'. Tsere has the pronunciation 'ai' and generally appears in transliteration with a horizontal line (a macron) above the letter 'e' indicating a pronunciation of the 'e' as in 'they', therefore '*Yēshua*', not 'Yeshua' as it is often written and pronounced.

The name **Yaishua** refers to nine people in the Old Testament. This name is identified in Strong's Concordance* (no. 3442) as '*Jeshua*' (meaning 'He will save').

* Thomas Nelson Publishers Inc., Nashville, Tennessee.

In Nehemiah 8:17 of the Hebrew text, '**Yaishua**' refers to the son of Nun.

The three Greek manuscripts used in this study all contain 'Iesous' (in Hebrews 4:8 and Acts 7:45*) in clear reference to 'Joshua', as most versions identify it in their texts. On all other occasions, each version translates 'Iesous' to 'Jesus'.

* Professor Franz Delitzsch's Hebrew New Testament contains 'Yᵉhoshua' in these two texts and '**Yaishua**' elsewhere.

In both of the above texts, the **KJV** retains **'Jesus'** and, in Acts 7:45, draws attention to Hebrews 4:8, which contains the margin note: 'i.e. *Joshua*'.

Acts 7:45 in the NASB contains 'Joshua' and contains the margin note: 'Gr., *Jesus*'.

Strong's Concordance also identifies the name under the reference '*Joshua*': 'See *Hosea, Hoshea, Jehoshuah, Jeshua, Jeshuah, Jesus, Osea, Oshea*.'

All these indicate that the Hebrew **Yaishua** is synonymous to **Yᵉhoshua** and the Greek **Iesous**.

One can imagine the confused response if the question posed by Agur in Proverbs 30:4-5 were to be asked of a mixed congregation of various Christian denominations today.

CVOT: 'Who has ascended into heaven and descended? Who has gathered the wind in His fists? Who has wrapped the waters in His garment? Who has established all the ends of the earth? *What is His name or His Son's name? Surely you know*! Every word of God is tested; He is a shield to those who take refuge in Him. Do not add to His words lest He reprove you and you be proved a liar' ('nor take away from them', Deuteronomy 4:2).

To successfully prosecute the claim that **it is** possible to factually determine this issue, some of the factors responsible for the disputed readings must be addressed. They are the following:

a) Differing interpretations of the source texts when being transmitted from the ancient Greek into English Bible versions.

b) Traditional doctrines overriding the literal meanings of the texts; in other words, the meaning of some passages have been contrived to accommodate preconceived doctrinal outcomes in stark contrast to the intended *literal* meanings in the ancient Greek codices.

c) Jewish customs identified in the texts that theologians have either been unaware of or have chosen to ignore, without which the true context of such passages cannot be accurately understood.

d) The literal scriptural evidence to be submitted herein is supported by the historical record and astronomical calculations, both of which support the integrity of the literal texts that form the basis of 'The Trial'. These literal meanings are consistent throughout and should never have been changed at the behest of theologians to comply with preconceived traditional beliefs.

e) The difference in the reckoning of time between the Jewish calendar and the Julian or Gregorian calendars has contributed to the confusion that exists in the differing doctrines believed today, leaving a blurred image of the days in question as in a double-exposed photograph. This is because the days recorded in the scriptures began and ended at sunset, whereas in the Julian/Gregorian calendars, they began and ended at midnight, as identified in the following diagram:

```
                   sunset    sunset    sunset    sunset    sunset
Jewish Calendar  →|_day 1__|_ day 2__|_day 3__|_day 4_|

                   midnight  midnight  midnight  midnight
Julian Calendar  →    |_day 1_|_day 2_ |_day 3__|_day 4_|
```

Regardless of which calendars are variously claimed should be used in a study such as this, the days must first be understood according to the Jewish calendar as they were at the time the events unfolded without the overlap of how our current calendar identifies them.

f) Another commonly overlooked but important factor is that the ancient *uncial* Greek texts used in this study did not contain the chapters, verses, or punctuation that currently appear in our bibles, neither was there any separation between the letters. A similar grouping of words in English would appear like this:

CURRENTCHAPTERSVERSESANDPUNCTUATION WEREADDEDLONGAFTERTHEANCIENTGREEK MANUSCRIPTSWEREWRITTEN.

It should come as no surprise that the arbitrary addition of these has had a profound influence upon the perceived context of how many texts are currently understood. They should never be relied upon to decide the context of any scripture, but they are an excellent innovation as a simple reference device and are invaluable for that purpose only.

g) When the fine print is translated in its original literal form, you may discover that your Bible(s) does not contain a particular word or passage that appears in the ancient Greek texts, which—had they been included—would have considerably influenced the way the texts were understood. The reason for this will either become obvious or will be explained as we proceed.

There is no doubt that the content of 'The Trial' will intrude upon **your** sincerely held beliefs, and you will be confronted with what will be termed herein as the 'tentacles of tradition'; however, you will be able to assess whether or not your own sincerely held doctrinal belief is consistent with what is actually written in the fine print of the ancient scriptural texts.

If personal experience is anything to go by, you will discover that these doctrinal tentacles will cause you considerable difficulty when you are challenged by the evidence to be submitted herein and will be harder to break free from than you can possibly imagine at this point.

Each of the three commonly believed doctrines under examination have emerged from disputed readings and are responsible for the deep schisms that have divided Christians throughout the ages, which have become entrenched as strongly held traditions.

Of course, traditions based upon scriptural truth should be held strongly; however, *scriptural truth does not change at the behest of theologians*, many of whom differ considerably from one another, which is apparent from the manifold doctrines in existence today.

It should be clearly understood that all references to the preconceived doctrines responsible for the systematic errors to be revealed in 'The Trial' are in no way intended to be personally directed at any sincere follower of these doctrines.

Since the accounts describing the death and resurrection of the Messiah, written in such graphic detail in the four Gospels of the New Testament almost 2,000 years ago, were copied into other languages (no original manuscripts are known to exist), conflicting doctrines, all of which claim to be true to those early accounts, have arisen within the ranks of sincere believers throughout the earth.

So complex and varied have the differences become that it is hard to believe that these death and resurrection accounts could all stem from the same source—the Bible.

As a result of these differing interpretations and for the purposes of this study, *a distinction will be made herein between 'the scriptures' and 'the Bible'.*

But do you think that God intended these divisions by inspiring the scriptures to be written? The apostle Paul obviously didn't think so.

CLNT: 'Now I am entreating you brethren through the name of our Lord, Jesus Christ, that all should be saying the same thing and there be no schisms among you, but you may be attuned to the same mind and the same opinion' (1 Corinthians 1:10).

Martin Luther identified many of the doctrinal errors taught by the Roman Catholic Church; however, so intricate was/is the web of deception that it would be naive to think that all errors at that time were, or have since been, identified. It is a fertile field for scrutiny.

An example of how the insertion of just one comma has affected the understanding of a scriptural passage, which has caused subsequent division between various groups of believers, appears in Luke 23:39-43.

CLNT: 'Now one of the hanged malefactors blasphemed Him . . . Yet answering, the other one, rebuking him averred . . . And he said to Jesus, "Be reminded of me, Lord, when ever Thou mayest be coming in Thy kingdom". And Jesus said to him: "Verily to you am I saying today, with Me shall you be in paradise."'

With the comma placed after 'today', it means that **Yaishua** made the promise on the day He died, 'today', and that the felon would join Him in paradise at a future time. On the other hand, if a comma was placed instead after 'saying', it would mean that **Yaishua** and the felon would both be in paradise on the day of their crucifixion.

One comma, two vastly different meanings—one true and the other false!

Leaving aside the facts:

i) The felon was requesting to be remembered when **Yaishua** returned to His kingdom—not to be in paradise on the day of His death.

ii) Crucifixion was intended to be a slow torturous death, evidenced by Pilate's surprise that **Yaishua** had died the same day He was crucified.

That was not the fate of the two malefactors crucified with **Yaishua,** whose legs were broken before they were taken away whilst their agonising suffering continued and to prevent anyone from attempting to rescue them during the hours of darkness. Remember that the next day began at sunset a short time later.

iii) Whereas **Yaishua** was buried shortly before sunset on the day He died and since He was roused from the dead three days and three nights after His death, He could not have taken the malefactor to paradise on the day He died.

iv) According to **Yaishua's** own words, He was to be buried for *three days and three nights* after He died, so He certainly didn't intend to convey to the believing malefactor that he would be with Him in paradise on the day He died.

We are also able to resolve the issue of the placement of the comma by turning elsewhere in the scriptures.

CLNT: 'And no one has ascended into heaven except Him Who descends out of heaven, the Son of Man(kind) Who is in heaven' (John 3:13).

Since John wrote these words long after **Yaishua** had ascended into heaven, clearly the felon was not yet with Him in paradise.

This was also alluded to by Paul in 1 Corinthians 15:20: 'Yet now Christ has been roused from among the dead, the Firstfruit of those who are reposing.'

As we have just observed, the scriptures are written in such a way that, where applicable, one passage or word may be used to interpret another, enabling us in many instances to identify errors and/or uncertain meanings, which are invaluable in correcting disputed readings.

CVOT: 'For instruction is added to instruction. Instruction to instruction; principle to principle . . . a little here, a little there' (Isaiah 28:9-10, 13).

CLNT: 'And we are having the prophetic word more confirmed, which you doing ideally are heeding . . . knowing this first, that no prophecy of Scripture at all is becoming its own interpretation' (2 Peter 1:19-20).

This principle is used throughout 'The Trial', making it unnecessary to superimpose doctrinal opinions over the ancient texts, which has been done in the formation of the traditional doctrines, as you will soon discover.

It is worth noting that when Paul preached to the Bereans, they examined the scriptures carefully to ascertain whether Paul was correct or not. As a result, many of them believed, both Jews and Gentiles.

CLNT: 'Now the brethren immediately sent out both Paul and Silas by night into Berea . . . coming along into the synagogue of the Jews . . . who receive the word with all eagerness, examining the Scriptures day by day to see if these have it thus. Many of them indeed believe and of the respectable Greek women and men not a few.'

The scriptures the Bereans were referring to were those of the Old Testament, and given the care taken in copying those texts from generation to generation, they would have been an accurate rendition of the original texts, unlike the English interpretations of the Greek manuscripts we currently read in most bibles, where liberties have been taken to conform the texts to preconceived beliefs.

Even so, it is evident that not all Bereans believed Paul's testimony. Clearly, from the same texts, some opted to cling to traditional doctrinal interpretations. You also may have cause to reflect on this issue as you examine 'the prosecution's' case.

It is often stated that the days in question are unimportant, however, truth is the sum of its individual parts; alter or remove one part, and you no longer have the (original) whole truth.

The times that these events took place were divinely *appointed times* (in Hebrew, *moadim*), as **Yaishua** confirmed in reference to His approaching death (Matthew 26:18).

The days on which these events took place are clearly identified in the fine print of the scriptures; when they are correctly read, they prevent the whole truth from being distorted into alternative 'new truths', which is exactly what 'The Trial' will endeavour to prove has happened.

Only the Creator of time can appoint such times, as Matthew alludes to.

CLNT: 'Now concerning that day and hour no one is aware, neither the messengers of the heavens, nor the Son; except the Father only' (Matthew 24:36; also Mark 13:32, Acts 1:7).

The claim that the days are unimportant is nothing more than an apologetic device to conceal the deficiency of these historic traditions.

The Concordant Interlinear Greek text has been provided to enable you to make an assessment of whether the facts are accurately provided in some of these key texts.

As a result of the foregoing, the prosecution states:

i) Many current versions of the Bible have corrupted the integrity of the ancient Greek texts relating to the death and resurrection of the Son of God, which is used in 'The Trial', in favour of traditional doctrines.

ii) This has been achieved by mistranslating words in the texts, by adding words to reinforce those mistranslations, and/or by omitting words, thereby obscuring the literal meaning of various passages, which are all critical factors in untangling this litany of errors.

Of course, it is one thing to make such claims, but quite another to prove them beyond all reasonable doubt, so without any further delay, let us begin 'The Trial'.

The Trial

Chapter One

The vast majority of Christians today base their belief that the Son of God died on Good Friday and was resurrected on Easter Sunday morning from what they have read in their bibles. This has resulted in the belief in either an AD 33 or 30 (33 or 30 CE) death and resurrection.

From the same biblical texts, a much smaller number believe that the crucifixion occurred on a Wednesday afternoon and the resurrection late on a Saturday afternoon, generally in AD 31 (31 CE).

It is of the utmost importance to realise that the events are not identified in either of those ways in the fine print of the ancient texts.

Because we have earlier identified three different versions of the truth (30, 31, 33 CE), one of which you undoubtedly subscribe to, we will need to examine the basis of each of these beliefs, both individually and collectively, as differences between them arise.

In this publication, the literal fine print is introduced first (with the exception of the first evidential 'exhibit') and then compared with the biblical versions and the doctrines that have emanated from them.

To clarify this basic issue, we will begin by comparing the overlapping times of the days of the three popular doctrines as they appear in both the Gregorian/Julian calendars and in the fine print of the ancient texts.

According to the Jewish calendar, Passover began after sunset on 14 Nisan and continued until the following sunset.
Annual festivals, like Passover, fell on different days each year.

However, according to the Julian and Gregorian calendars, this meant Passover was observed on parts of *two days*: from sunset to midnight on one day and from midnight to sunset the following day.

The **33 and 30*** CE doctrines claim:

i) The Last Supper took place in the evening of *Holy Thursday*. Bear in mind that according to the Julian and Gregorian calendars, Thursday began at midnight, approximately twenty hours before the memorial meal, whereas 14 Nisan began at *sunset on Thursday*.

ii) Therefore, according to the Julian calendar, the crucifixion would have taken place during *the day following* the Passover memorial meal, *Good Friday*. However, according to the Jewish calendar, *the crucifixion* would have occurred on *the same day* as the memorial meal, the Passover on 14 Nisan.

iii) The resurrection took place at dawn on Easter *Sunday*, which most bibles identify as *the first day of the week*.

iv) This would have to be *16 Nisan*.

* The differences between the **33** and **30** CE belief are studied in a later chapter.

The **31** CE doctrine claims:

i) The Passover memorial meal was eaten after sunset on a *Tuesday*.

ii) The crucifixion took place *the day after the Tuesday evening* Passover memorial meal (Julian/Gregorian calendar). However, according to the Jewish calendar, *Wednesday* would still have been *14 Nisan* (until sunset).

iii) The resurrection took place late on a *Saturday* afternoon before sunset.

iv) In that case, it would have been *17 Nisan*.

These raise the questions:

Did **Yaishua** die on *Friday, 14 Nisan,* and did His resurrection occur on *Sunday, 16 Nisan, in 33 or 30* CE?

Or did He die on *Wednesday, 14 Nisan,* and was He resurrected on *Saturday, 17 Nisan 31* CE?

Consequently, we are not simply dealing with differences in terms of a few hours but *in years, plus a few hours*! The timeline diagrams in chapter 4 clearly illustrate these issues.

One thing is certain about these beliefs, including your own—**they cannot all be true.** In fact, of these three popular doctrines, there is the possibility—the almost unthinkable—that *all of them may be false*!

Another certainty is that the truth of these matters cannot be decided by a majority vote, nor can it be measured solely by *sincerity,* for it is possible to be *sincerely wrong* about all manner of issues.

Exhibit 1

Let us begin by finding out the basis of these widely divergent claims by submitting Matthew 28:1 as it appears in the three popular versions selected to represent most current Bible versions throughout 'The Trial'.

KJV: 'In the end of the sabbath, as it began to dawn toward the first day of the week . . .'
NASB: 'Now late on the Sabbath, as it began to dawn toward the first day of the week . . .'
RSV: 'Now after the sabbath, toward the first day of the week . . .'

Regardless of whether you believe in a Sunday morning (30 or 33 CE) or Saturday afternoon (31 CE) resurrection, the *only* conclusion you can come to when reading these three versions is that Matthew is referring to *two consecutive days*: Saturday, the seventh-day Sabbath, and Sunday, the first day of the week.

You no doubt think this is so obvious that it is absurd to even mention; however, after you have finished studying the evidence submitted throughout 'The Trial', you will have good cause to reconsider that view.

Whichever doctrine you subscribe to, there *appears to be* little problem in understanding this text, but if that is the case, how is it that from this one passage, different interpretations of the days and years of the death and resurrection have developed?

The above interpretations in the **KJV** and **NASB** are ambiguous at best because both clearly state that the events took place '*in the end of*' or '*late on*' the *Sabbath*—in other words, on or about sunset on Saturday.

In an attempt to lead sincere Bible students to believe the traditional morning resurrection on the *first day of the week*, the context has been altered by the insertion of the word '*day*'—non-existent in the ancient texts—supported by the interpretation of the Greek word '*(epi) phoskouse*', literally '*on lighting/lighting up*', as '*dawn*' the following morning.

However, because these days *all ended at sunset*, the texts in reality indicate that the events occurred in the period *before sunset*, but as you will discover, this is not as the redactors variously claim.

On the other hand, those who understand that the text is referring to a time towards the end of the day before sunset of the seventh-day Sabbath (in 31 CE) believe that the resurrection took place at that time.

It is obviously a physical impossibility for it to be about sunset on one day and sunrise the following morning at the same time, yet this text has been interpreted either one way or the other by the different doctrines under scrutiny herein.

The prosecution will reveal that the context of this passage has been seriously compromised and, *because the meaning of words are resolved by the context in which they are used*, will explain and correct the ambiguity that exists in current interpretations of Matthew's Gospel.

The **RSV** is more definitive but has taken the passage completely out of context, as we will soon discover.

Although this is an obvious example of Sir Frederick Kenyon's allusion to a disputed reading, it is difficult to understand how he could have concluded that no fundamental doctrine of the Christian faith rests upon such a difference in the reading of this text since it has led to such widespread uncertainty and often bitter disagreement.

However, the problems associated with these different doctrinal interpretations are far more extensive than those that we have examined thus far, so how do we determine with certainty when the death and resurrection of the Messiah took place?

It appears that all we have to do is find whether the resurrection occurred *after* the seventh-day Sabbath as the day dawned on 'the first day of the week', as one interpretation proposes, or '*in the end of*' or '*late on*' the seventh-day Sabbath before sunset, as others claim.

Or is there another credible option? To successfully prosecute these issues, we must first establish a literal understanding of the times in question: the days from Pesach/Passover to Shavuoth/Pentecost.

Chapter Two

Exhibit 2

CVOT: 'These are the appointed seasons of **Yahweh**, the holy meetings, which you are to proclaim at *the appointed times*: *In the first month* ['Aviv' in Exodus 13:4; 'Nisan' in Nehemiah 2:1], *on the fourteenth day of the month* between the evening hours, *is the Passover of Yahweh. On the fifteenth day of this month* is the celebration of *unleavened cakes* [in Hebrew, 'matzot'] to **Yahweh**. *Seven days* shall you eat unleavened cakes. *On the first day**1* you shall come to have a holy meeting, when you shall do no occupational work at all; you shall bring a fire offering to **Yahweh** [for] *seven days. On the seventh day**2* is a holy meeting . . . *From the morrow after the first sabbath**3* . . . You will count off for yourselves *from the morrow after the first sabbath,**3* from the day you bring the sheaf of the wave offering, there shall be *seven flawless sabbaths**4* . . . *Until the morrow after the seventh sabbath**5* you shall count fifty days' (Leviticus 23:5-16; abbreviated, with emphasis, italics and parenthetical elements added to specifically identify the issues under scrutiny).

The above notations referring to the day of Passover, the days of Unleavened Bread, Wave Sheaf, and Pentecost are easily identified in the following timeline diagrams:

Passover	Day 1*[1]	Day 2	Day 3	Day 4	Day 5	Day 6	Day 7*[2]
14 Nisan	15 Nisan	16 Nisan	17 Nisan	18 Nisan	19 Nisan	20 Nisan	21 Nisan

*[1] The fifteenth day of the first month (verse 6), Aviv/Nisan, is identified in verse 7 as the first day of the seven days of the Festival of Unleavened Bread.

*[2] Verse 8 identifies the seventh day of the seven days of the Unleavened Bread Festival as the twenty-first day of the month.

	Day 1	2	3	4	5	6	Day 7*[4]
First Sabbath*[3]	Wave Sheaf						First Sabbath after Wave Sheaf

*[3] The first seventh-day Sabbath after Passover.

*[4] The second seventh-day Sabbath after Passover, the first of the seven 'flawless' seventh-day Sabbaths between Wave Sheaf and Pentecost.

The **CVOT** has included the reading *'first'* from a **Septuagint (LXX)** insertion, which does not appear in the Hebrew texts but is supported by the New Testament; hence, it plays an important part in understanding the intended method of enumerating these days.

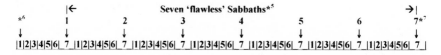

*[5] Seven seven-day periods, each ending on a seventh-day Sabbath.

*[6] Wave Sheaf.

*[7] The seventh of the seven Sabbaths, the day before Pentecost.

Leviticus 23:15:

KJV: 'seven sabbaths shall be complete . . .'

NASB: 'seven complete sabbaths . . .'

RSV: 'seven full weeks . . .'

Hebrew: 'sheva shabbatot(h) ('temiymot') . . .' This literally means 'seven sabbaths' (flawless/complete/perfect ones).

Leviticus 23:16:

KJV, NASB, and RSV: 'After the seventh sabbath . . .'
Hebrew: 'hashabbat(h) hash⁽ᵉ⁾viyit(h) . . .' This literally reads as 'the sabbath, the seventh (one)'.

It is clear that the word 'weeks' in verse 15 of the **RSV** should have been translated as 'seven (full) sabbaths' since in verse 16 it acknowledges that Pentecost occurs on the day following the counting of the seventh Sabbath, not the seventh week.

Unfortunately, those versions that contain 'weeks' obscure the true context that each seven-day period following Wave Sheaf ended in a seventh-day Sabbath, seven of which were to be counted before the day of the Pentecost.

Consequently, you can see that there is a distinct difference between 'seven sabbaths' and 'seven weeks' when they are literally translated.

The text clearly defines a specific difference between *the first day* of the days of Unleavened Bread (verse 7) on 15 Nisan and *the (first seventh-day) Sabbath* immediately preceding Wave Sheaf (verse 11). We will discover that this is also clearly defined in the fine print of the New Testament texts.

Those who believe that the 'first day' and this 'first sabbath' were both referring to 15 Nisan, as some did and still do, count(ed) seven weeks to Pentecost, not seven Sabbaths as literally instructed, from the following day. This meant that the fiftieth day, Pentecost, fell on a different day of the week each year.

On the other hand, those who count(ed) seven seven-day periods with each seven-day period ending in a seventh-day Sabbath, as others did and still do, always observe(d) Pentecost on the day following the seventh of the (seventh-day) Sabbaths after Wave Sheaf.

The argument that each seven-day period is a week completely misses the point. The issue is that when these scriptures are *not literally* translated as they were intended to be, not only is the integrity of the context of a particular text affected but they may also adversely compromise other associated texts elsewhere, which will be demonstrated to be an all too common occurrence in the texts under scrutiny.

This is important because these texts were intended to be wholly cohesive and not fragmented by disputable interpretations.

Chapter Three

Exhibit 3

The fine print of the literal text of Matthew 28:1

With this in mind, let us continue our study of Matthew's account with a transliteration of the Greek text, followed by a literal translation, and compare them word for word with the sample versions we have already examined.

CLNT interlinear Greek text (CLNTG)

1	ˉ ΟΨΕ	ΔΕ	ϹΑΒΒΑΤΩΝ	ΤΗ	ΕΠΙΦΩϹΚΟΥϹΗ	ΕΙϹ	ΜΙΑΝ	ϹΑΒΒΑΤΩΝ	ΗΛΘΕΝ
	evening	YET	OF-SABBATHS	to-THE	ON-LIGHTING lighting-up	INTO	ONE	OF-SABBATHS	CAME

Transliteration: 'Opse de sabbaton te epiphoskouse eis mian sabbaton.'
CLNT: 'Now it is the **evening** of the sabbaths at the lighting up into one of the sabbaths.'

KJV: 'In the **end** of the sabbath . . .'
NASB: 'Now **late** on the Sabbath . . .'
RSV: 'Now **after** the sabbath . . .'

Opse—this form of the Greek word appears three times in the New Testament; using 'a little here, a little there', the true meaning of all three becomes absolutely clear.

> i)   **CLNT:** 'And whenever it came to be evening (opse), they went out, outside the city. And going by in the morning . . .' (Mark 11:19-20).

KJV: 'And when even (opse) was come, he went out of the city. And in the morning . . .'

NASB: 'And whenever evening (opse) came, they would go out of the city. And as they were passing by in the morning . . .'

RSV: 'And when evening (opse) came they went out of the city. As they passed by in the morning . . .'

There can be no doubt that this text is describing a time late in the day before sunset (early evening), when **Yaishua** and His disciples left Jerusalem while there was sufficient light for them to travel safely to the place where they intended to spend the night.

> ii)   **CLNT, KJV, and RSV:** 'Watch therefore—for you do not know when the master of the house will come, in the evening (opse), or at midnight, or at cockcrow, or in the morning' (Mark 13:35).

NASB: 'Therefore, be on the alert—for you do not know when the master of the house is coming, whether in the evening (opse), at midnight, or at cockcrowing, or in the morning.'

In this passage, 'opse' is referring to the first of the watches that took place—from sunset to morning—and obviously cannot be construed to mean the following morning under any circumstance. You can plainly see that in both of these texts, the sample versions respectively validate 'opse' as 'even' or 'evening'.

Mark also identifies 'opsias' in 1:32:

CLNT: 'Now evening ['opsias'] coming on, *when the sun sets . . .*'

It should be quite clear that the context of Matthew's use of 'opse' was no different and did not intend to convey the meaning 'after' or 'dawn' the following day.

This evidential exhibit is the first example of the widespread practice of interpreting words to suit a preconceived doctrinal understanding of the texts and reveals that all these scriptural references to 'opse' (or 'opsias') indicate that they *never* referred to a time later than evening.

Because 'opse' was meant to convey the meaning 'evening' throughout, the claims that it refers to the next morning are invalid; therefore, 'the first day of the week' resurrection is scripturally untrue. (But it is biblically correct!)

The ramifications of this, after just one evidential exhibit of the fine print, should make for interesting reading as we proceed, which will immediately become even more certain with the evidence now to be introduced.

Chapter Four

Exhibit 4

'Sabbath' or 'week'?

CLNTG

1	`OΨЄ	ΔЄ	CΑΒΒΑΤѠN	TH	ЄΠΙΦѠCKOYCH	ЄIC	MIΑN	CΑΒΒΑΤѠN	HΛΘЄN
	evening	YET	OF-SABBATHS	to-THE	ON-LIGHTING lighting-up	INTO	ONE	OF-SABBATHS	CAME

Transliteration: 'Opse de **sabbaton** te epiphoskouse eis mian **sabbaton**.'

CLNT: 'Now it is the evening of the **sabbaths** at the lighting up into one of the **sabbaths**.'

KJV: 'Now late on the **sabbath**, as it began to dawn toward the first day of **the week** . . .'

NASB: 'Now late on the **Sabbath**, as it began to dawn toward the first day of **the week** . . .'

RSV: 'Now after the **sabbath**, toward the first day of **the week** . . .'

Just as English adopts words from other languages, so also have the Greek texts adopted words from Hebrew and Aramaic readings.

The Greek word 'sabbaton' was adopted from Hebrew, as Strong's Concordance confirms:* '[no. 4521] 'sabbaton'; of Heb. Or. [no. 7676]; the Sabbath (i.e. Shabbath)'.

'Shabbaton' is a Hebrew word which describes a sacred time of rest, associated with a Sabbath. (Langenscheidt Hebrew-English Dictionary to the Old Testament by Dr. Karl Feyerabend)

* Strong's adds the following statement after 'Shabbath': 'Day of weekly repose from secular avocations (also the observance or institution itself); by extens. A sennight, i.e. the interval between two sabbaths; likewise the plural in all the above applications:- sabbath (day), week.'

Strong's identifies 'sabbaton' nine times as 'week' in the New Testament texts. Consequently, it makes only one reference to 'sabbath' in Matthew 28:1, with the second 'sabbaton' identified as the word 'week'.

The reason for this is explained in the publisher's preface:

> The fruit of 35 years of labor by Dr. Strong and more than 100 colleagues, his volume has since become the most widely used concordance ever *compiled from the King James Version of the Bible*, still the standard English version of the Bible. (italics added)

This reveals that Dr Strong and his colleagues were predisposed to translate the second 'sabbaton' as 'week' from the King James Version, rather than uphold the integrity of its literal meaning as demonstrated by the fine print of the Greek scriptures, which were known at the time it was published.

The King James Version is dedicated to 'the most high and mighty King James . . . defender of the faith'; with particular regard to the Good Friday death and Easter Sunday resurrection in spite of King James's affiliation to Protestantism, the faith he was held to be the defender of originated from the Roman Catholic Church many centuries earlier.

Consequently, Strong's added explanation in no. 4521 has more to do with the interpretation contained in the **KJV** than what is literally written in the ancient Greek texts.* There has never been an either-or option for Matthew's second use of the word 'sabbaton'. It was always intended to mean 'sabbaths', not 'week'.

* In reference to the **KJV**, the Encyclopaedia Britannica (15th edition) states: 'In particular, the Greek text of the New Testament, which they used as their base, was a poor one. The great early Greek codices were not then known or available and Hellenistic papyri, which were to shed light on the common Greek dialect, had not yet been discovered.'

Notwithstanding the above comments, the meaning of the word 'sabbaton' is a matter of *mistranslation*, not one of a different Greek text.

The second 'sabbaton' in Matthew's account, 'one of the sabbaths', is plural for a very good reason—it is referring to one of the seventh-day Sabbaths between Passover and Pentecost.

This 'correction' of the second 'sabbaton' to 'week' is in reality saying that '*Sabbath*' means '*Sunday*' because the redactor's doctrinal belief so demands.

In the English language, a Sabbath day identifies just that—whether it is an annual Sabbath or weekly Sabbath, it is and can only mean *Sabbath*. This is also true of shabbat(h) in Hebrew.

How then could it be any different in the Greek language, where it is claimed to mean both '*sabbath*' and '*week*' significantly only on the occasions where '(*one of the*) *sabbaths*' appears in the ancient texts?

Perhaps, rather than recognize it as the translation 'week', it would be better described as a 'weak' translation!

In spite of Strong's learned opinion, it is an undeniable fact that:

   i) The Greek word 'sabbaton' *appears twice* in Matthew 28:1 in the Greek codices.

   ii) All three sample versions acknowledge that the first appearance of 'sabbaton' in this passage means '*sabbath*' by translating it as such: '*in the end/late/after the sabbath*'.

   iii) The *second* 'sabbaton' has clearly been *replaced (or 'corrected')* with 'week' solely for preconceived doctrinal reasons.

In **exhibit 1**, attention was drawn to the ambiguous way that Matthew 28:1 has been interpreted, which pales into insignificance when compared to this glaring example of the licence taken in altering the fine print, which is nothing less than 'subterfugion'* by substitution.

* 'Subterfuge', 'an evasive device, as used in discussion or argument; action taken or manouvres made, to evade, conceal or obscure' (Chambers Concise Dictionary. Chambers Harrap Publishers Ltd, 7 Hopetoun Crescent, Edinburgh, EH7 4AY).

Most bibles have not only modified the consistent and only true meaning of 'sabbaton', which is 'sabbath', but they have also added or misinterpreted other words to accommodate the interpolation* 'week'.

* 'Interpolation', 'to insert a word or passage in a book or manuscript especially in order to mislead; to tamper with, to corrupt by spurious insertions; to insert, interpose, interject' (published by W&R Chambers Ltd).

On the other hand, the prosecution asserts that the two sabbatons were intended to mean two Sabbaths. Why else would the authors of the Gospels, in describing the events in terms and language used by the early Jewish believers who were the original recipients of the reports, have written it in such a way that resulted in the early copiers to record it *twice* as 'sabbaton' ('sabbath')? If the second 'sabbaton' was intended to mean 'the first day of the week', the appropriate words would have been used.

Of course, it is possible for *annual Sabbaths* to fall on any day of the week; however, this text is not referring to an annual Sabbath, as these sample versions have clearly revealed by inserting 'week' to replace the correct translation, 'sabbaths'.

Had it been understood to be referring to an annual Sabbath, it would have been translated as the textual '*as it began to dawn toward one of the sabbaths*' or '*the first sabbath*', which would have altogether compromised the credibility of the 'first day of the week' redaction.

Other contributing reasons the passage was interpreted this way are:

i) as a direct consequence of the arbitrary insertion of a new chapter into the narrative (non-existent in the uncial Greek texts), which compels the sincere student to believe the passage is referring to two consecutive days, the last of which must be the day following the seventh-day Sabbath, the unscriptural 'first day of the week'.

ii) either ignorance of or scant regard given to the Jewish nature of the texts. You will discover that unless this latter issue is recognised, there cannot be an accurate understanding of this and other related texts.

iii) the practice of replacing the literal meaning of words in the Greek texts, adding to them, or completely omitting them to enable the perpetuation of the traditional 'first day of the week' doctrine.

Considering the length of time that this question has been studied, it seems incredible that most Christians have been (and still are) completely unaware that 'sabbaths' ('sabbaton') appears twice in this passage and those that do give no credence to the fact that it has been corrected to conform to a meaning quite different to that demanded by the context.

These aspects will be looked at in greater detail shortly.

To understand the correct context and explain why two sabbatons were written in the ancient texts to literally mean two Sabbaths, we need to expand this passage by reading it in conjunction with the preceding verse (Matthew 27:66) and by removing the arbitrarily inserted Matthew 28:1.

CLNT: 'Now they being gone secure the tomb with the detail now it is the evening of *the sabbaths** ('opse de sabbaton')

At the lighting up into *one of the sabbaths* ('eis mian sabbaton') came Mary Magdalene.'

* The **CLNT** identifies this as 'sabbaths'; however, the same day elsewhere in the New Testament is identified in the singular 'sabbath', which will become apparent as we proceed.

In the above text, separate paragraphs have been used to emphasize the correct context of the two sabbatons, which as you can see is.

The sealing of the tomb was completed by the detail of soldiers towards the end of *the annual* festival Sabbath (15 Nisan) at the time Matthew identified as 'the evening of the sabbaths' ('opse de sabbaton').

Following this, the women returned on a later day to observe the tomb close to sunset 'at the lighting up into one of the sabbaths', which we will reveal was *before* the second 'sabbaton' had begun, *not at dawn*.

Let us pause right here and take stock of what has just been stated because if you have doubted that the tentacles of tradition have you firmly in their grasp, this should bring it into clear focus!

You will agree that the above context completely changes the way this text has been historically interpreted, the magnitude of which is a complete game changer *if it is true* (and the purpose of 'The Trial' is to prove beyond reasonable doubt that this is the way the truth of these matters should have been correctly understood), because it exposes the fact that Matthew was distinctly identifying *two Sabbath days*—the first being *the festival Sabbath* and the second *the seventh-day Sabbath*, **not** *the first day of the week*.

Therefore, these two Sabbaths *did not occur on consecutive days*, which all three doctrines rely on for credibility, and neither should they have done so if **Yaishua's** words are to be believed, which will be explained as we proceed.

Furthermore, if the prosecution can prove beyond all reasonable doubt that the second 'sabbaton' means *the seventh-day Sabbath* and not the first day of the week, not only are the three doctrines under scrutiny invalid, but it also raises serious questions regarding the veracity of not only the three sample versions used throughout 'The Trial' but also every other Bible version that has replaced 'one of the sabbaths' with the spurious 'first day of the week'.

Perhaps it might be helpful to proceed by imagining that the three doctrines—30 CE, 31 CE, and 33 CE—are represented by jigsaws, depicting the details of the same event in significantly different ways.

These traditional 'jigsaws' have been historically assembled on the following basis:

33 and 30 CE

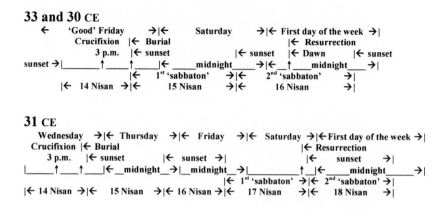

31 CE

The prosecution charges that each of these beliefs have caused the original picture to become so distorted they no longer accurately represent its original appearance.

In the process of restoring the original picture, the prosecution inserted one of the jigsaw pieces into its correct place according to the earliest of the ancient Greek 'instruction books' available:

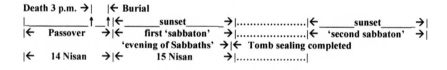

Chapter Five

Exhibit 5

Dawn or 'lighting up'?

CLNTG

1	˙ ΟΨΕ	ΔΕ	CΑΒΒΑΤωΝ	ΤΗ	ΕΠΙΦωCΚΟΥCΗ	ΕΙC	ΜΙΑΝ	CΑΒΒΑΤωΝ	ΗΛΘΕΝ
	evening	YET	OF-SABBATHS	to-THE	ON-LIGHTING lighting-up	INTO	ONE	OF-SABBATHS	CAME

Transliteration: 'Opse de sabbaton te **epiphoskouse** eis mian sabbaton.'

CLNT: 'Now it is the evening of the sabbaths at the **lighting up** into one of the sabbaths.'

KJV: 'In the end of the sabbath, **as it began to dawn** . . .'

NASB: 'Now late on the Sabbath, **as it began to dawn** . . .'

RSV: 'Now after the sabbath, **toward** the first day of the week . . .'

To demonstrate what Matthew meant by '*lighting up*', the prosecution again refers you to the principle of 'a little here, a little there' by drawing your attention to the literal meaning of Luke 23:54 as it appears in the ancient texts.

CLNTG

КΑΙΗΗΜΕΡΑΗΝΠΑΡΑCΚΕΥΗ 80
54 AND   THE DAY   it-WAS OF-preparation
A 0.   A *omits* AND
СΚΑΙCΑΒΒΑΤΟΝΕΠΕΦШСΚΕ 200
AND   SABBATH   ON-LIGHTED

CLNT: 'And it was the day of preparation and **a sabbath lighted up** (**'sabbaton epiphosken'**).'

KJV: 'And that day was the preparation and a sabbath **drew on**.'
NASB: 'And that day was the preparation and a Sabbath **was about to begin**.'
RSV: 'It was the day of Preparation and the sabbath **was beginning**.'

The Greek word 'phos' means 'light'. Strong's no. 5457 states: 'Luminousness (in the widest application, nat. or artif., abstr. or concr., lit. or fig.):- fire, light.'*

* The combination of fire (flame) to produce light accurately describes the custom of *lighting lamps* prior to Sabbath days.

If your Bible makes no mention of 'light' in this passage, this will again test the firm hold that the tentacles of tradition have over you. This will be dealt with in more detail shortly.

It is surely not possible that the redactors were unaware of the existence of 'light' ('epi*phos*ken') in the text because it appears in all three of the ancient Greek codices.

One has to ask, why was the fine print deliberately omitted, and how are sincere Bible students ever going to be able to correctly connect the dots if the fine print doesn't even appear in their bibles?

This omission simply illuminates the fact that where Jewish customs and/or practices exist in the texts, the redactors had/have no idea what they were actually referring to or thought they were inconsequential and paraphrased them.

This failure to insert the literal reference to 'a sabbath lighted up' into modern bibles has kept sincere Bible students in the dark not only about the enlightenment that Luke's account provides but equally so of Matthew's reference to 'lighting up' before the second 'sabbaton'/'sabbath'.

If the scriptural principle of 'a little here, a little there' had been applied, it would have shed much needed light on the similar time of day in both Matthew 28:1 and Luke 23:54, which would have resulted in the recognition of the important connection and seamless harmony of these two passages. This would have enabled the correct identification that the texts were both referring to the time immediately before sunset, when these two Sabbaths were lighted up.

The **RSV** appears to have been completely in the dark with these two texts since it omits any reference to 'light' in both Matthew's and Luke's Gospels, which is unsurprising really given the earlier alteration of 'evening' ('opse') to 'after' in Matthew 28:1 to reinforce the interpretation of the text.

In this passage, the New World Translation* includes a reference to '*light*', which—although it appears in an obscure way—does indicate that the fine print contained 'epiphosken': 'Now it was the day of Preparation, and *the evening light of the sabbath was approaching.*'

Insight On The Scriptures,* volume 2, page 831 states: 'According to rabbinic sources, in the time that Jesus was on earth three trumpet blasts at about the ninth hour, or three o'clock, on Friday afternoon announced the Sabbath day's approach. At this, all work and business were to cease, *the Sabbath lamp was lit*, and festive garments were put on. Then three more blasts indicated that Sabbath had actually begun.' (Italics added)

* Both publications are produced by the Watchtower Bible and Tract Society of New York, Inc. International Bible Students Association, Brooklyn, New York, U.S.A.

As with the last exhibit, this again demonstrates how one mistranslated text leads to further errors elsewhere and that the texts have been translated according to the misunderstood context of 'the first day of the week' doctrine, as you will continue to see as we proceed.

We have now clearly identified that *'the sabbath lighted up'* in Luke 23:54 when the burial was completed *was the beginning* of the first 'sabbaton' in Matthew 28:1 and that Matthew identified *the end of that day* when the sealing of the tomb had been completed as *'the evening of the sabbaths'*.

The original jigsaw now begins to look like this:

```
sunset              sunset              sunset   sunset           sunset                          sunset
↑_____14 Nisan_____↑_____15 Nisan_____↑......↑← Lev. 23:15  →↑←      Wave Sheaf       →↑
       Passover           |← 1st sabbaton →|     |← 2nd sabbaton →|←      Lev. 23:11           →|
                          | festival Sabbath    |........|← first Sabbath →|←'morrow after 1st sabb.' →|
'a Sabbath lighted up'→|  even. of Sabbaths→|        |← 'lighting up into one of the Sabbaths'
   Luke 23:54              Matthew 27:66           |← Resurrection, Matthew 28:1
   Burial completed →|                             |← Sealing of tomb completed
```

Chapter Six

Exhibit 6

Eis: 'into'

CLNTG

1	˝ OYЄ	ΔЄ	CΛΒΒΛΤωΝ	ΤΗ	ЄΠΙΦωCΚΟΥCΗ	ЄΙC	ΜΙΛΝ	CΛΒΒΛΤωΝ	ΗΛΘЄΝ
	evening	YET	OF-SABBATHS	to-THE	ON-LIGHTING lighting-up	INTO	ONE	OF-SABBATHS	CAME

Transliteration: 'Opse de sabbaton te epiphoskouse **eis** mian sabbaton.'

CLNT: 'Now it is the evening of the sabbaths at the lighting up **into** one of the sabbaths.'

KJV: 'Now in the end of the sabbath, as it began to dawn **toward** the first day of the week . . .'

NASB: 'Now late on the Sabbath, as it began to dawn **toward** the first day of the week . . .'

RSV: 'Now after the sabbath, **toward** the first day of the week . . .'

*Eis** is used in Matthew's account in the sense of approaching, 'on the cusp of entering into'.

* Used in the word *'eisegesis'*, reading a meaning *into* a text, whereas *exegesis* is based upon a critical analysis of a text.

This is something we have already witnessed in 'The Trial' and will continue to do as we proceed.

All three of the sample versions are in agreement with this by translating 'eis' as *'toward'*. Had the next day been the first day of the week, it would not have started until sunset, and since the text indicates that it was toward that time, it should not have been construed to mean *'dawn'* the next morning.

Chapter Seven

Exhibit 7

'One' or 'first'?

CLNTG

1	˘ ΟΨΕ	ΔΕ	CΑΒΒΑΤΩΝ	ΤΗ	ΕΠΙΦΩCΚΟΥCΗ	ΕΙC	ΜΙΑΝ	CΑΒΒΑΤΩΝ	ΗΛΘΕΝ
	evening	YET	OF-SABBATHS	to-THE	ON-LIGHTING lighting-up	INTO	ONE	OF-SABBATHS	CAME

Transliteration: 'Opse de sabbaton te epiphoskouse eis **mian** sabbaton.'

CLNT: 'Now it is the evening of the sabbaths at the lighting up into **one** of the sabbaths.'

KJV: 'In the end of the sabbath, as it began to dawn toward **the first** day of the week . . .'

NASB: 'Now late on the Sabbath, as it began to dawn toward **the first** day of the week . . .'

RSV: 'Now after the sabbath, toward **the first** day of the week . . .'

As you can see, each of the sample versions translate 'mian' as 'first'. They do so on each occasion that it appears in the Gospel accounts (five times) in reference to the resurrection and once each in Acts

(20:7), 1 Corinthians (16:2), and Titus (3:10), yet on each of the other fifty-five times it appears in the New Testament, it is translated as 'one'.

It should be apparent to you that even if the Greek language developed in such a way that 'mia(n)' had a secondary meaning ('first') only where it appeared literally as 'one of the sabbaths', how could it then cause 'sabbaton' ('sabbaths') to take on a new identity also, 'week', solely to conform to a religious doctrine?

This certainly is not the case; therefore, you would be right in believing that such a concept is absurd and that changing the correct meaning, 'one' to 'first', is simply an interpretation to accommodate the preconceived doctrinally inspired 'first (day) of the week'. This is a further example of how one mistranslation ('one' to 'first') leads to another ('sabbaths' to 'week') or others.

This is why it was necessary for Strong's Concordance (no. 3391) to once again give an either-or option, 'mia', 'irreg. fem. of no. 1520; one or first', as they did with 'sabbaton' and 'week'.

On the other hand, Strong's Concordance identifies 'proton/protos' as 'first' everywhere it appears throughout the New Testament where 'first' is demanded by the text (144 times). They are never interchanged with 'one' ('mian').

Strong's no. 4412 states: 'proton . . . firstly (in time, place, order, or importance):- before, at the beginning, best, chiefly, first (of all).'

Furthermore, the Greek words (in parentheses) that appear in Mark 16:9 are:

CLNT: 'Now rising, in the morning in the first sabbath ('prote sabbatou'), He appeared first ('proton') to Mary Magdalene.'

Instead of accepting that Mark 16:9 reveals that 'one of the sabbaths' ('mia ton sabbaton', verse 2) and 'first sabbath' ('prote sabbatou', verse 9) are referring to the same Sabbath, both verses are identified as *the first day of the week* in the sample versions, a clear alteration to the literally intended meaning.

There are several aspects to this:

i) In the Gospels, 'mia(n) sabbaton' was used in a general context to identify one of the seventh-day Sabbaths between Passover and Pentecost.

ii) It is important to note that 'one of the sabbaths' in the Gospel accounts identifies the first one of the seventh-day Sabbaths to occur after Passover, as Mark 16:9 reveals. Obviously, when referring to a series of Sabbaths, one of them must be the first.

This text also demolishes the notion that the resurrection occurred on either a *Sunday morning* or a Saturday afternoon because it refers to a *post-resurrection Saturday morning* encounter with Mary Magdalene.

iii) However, both Acts 20:7 and 1 Corinthians 16:2 identify 'one of the Sabbaths' in a different context, which in the next chapters will reveal the importance of consistently translating these texts literally, thus enabling the 'a little here, a little there' principle to be consistently applied.

To systematically alter it to 'first sabbath' throughout would require both texts to also be incorrectly inflicted with the same interpretation, as has been achieved with the illusory 'first day of the week' in both of these texts.

iv) When Mark wished to identify 'the first day', he wrote it this way: 'And on the first day ['prote emera'] of unleavened bread . . .' (Mark 14:12, **CLNT**), which would have also been written in 16:2 and 9 had it been intended to convey the meaning 'first day (of the week)', not 'mian sabbaton' or 'prote sabbatou'.

No matter how fine a point you believe is being made, the prosecution reaffirms its commitment to the importance of translating the texts literally. Because the contextual meaning of 'mia(n)' in the source texts is 'one', it must consistently be literally translated as such to enable the correct context to be understood.

It *is* certain that on neither occasion was Mark responsible for the spurious 'first day of the week' interpolation, neither were the other authors where it has been inserted into their accounts.

If it does nothing else, this demonstrates the determination of the redactors to force a doctrinally biased 'first day of the week' into the narrative *regardless of what words appear in the Greek codices.*

By inserting these incorrect interpretations into the biblical texts, the fine print has been altered to such an extent that it is no longer apparent to sincere students/believers, leading them to perpetuate these spurious traditional doctrines.

They may be biblically correct, but they do not factually represent the meaning of the texts in the ancient Greek manuscripts, hence the differentiation made between *the scriptures* and *the Bible* in the introduction to 'The Trial'.

As the prosecution has previously revealed the true literal meanings of 'sabbaton' as 'sabbath', 'opse' as 'evening', 'eis' as 'into', 'mian' as 'one', and 'prote' as 'first', you should by now be able to discern that these changes have been made solely to accommodate the preordained theology of a 'first day of the week' resurrection.

Chapter Eight

Exhibit 8

Counting the days between Passover and Pentecost

Part 1:

Did Paul observe the seventh-day Sabbath or the 'first day of the week'?

CLNTG

7	ΠΕΝΤΕ	ΟΠΟΥ	ΔΙΕΤΡΙΨΑΜΕΝ	ΗΜΕΡΑϹ	ΕΠΤΑ	ΕΝ	ΔΕ	ΤΗ	ΜΙΑ	ΤΩΝ
	FIVE	THE-?-where the-where	WE-tarry	DAYS	SEVEN	IN	YET	THE	ONE	OF-THE

ϹΑΒΒΑΤΩΝ	ϹΥΝΗΓΜΕΝΩΝ	ΗΜΩΝ	ΚΛΑϹΑΙ	ΑΡΤΟΝ	Ο	ΠΑΥΛΟϹ
SABBATHS	OF-HAVING-*been*-TOGETHER-LED of-having-*been*-assembled	US	TO-BREAK	BREAD	THE	PAUL

CLNT: 'Yet we sail off from Philippi **after the days of unleavened bread** . . . Now **on one of the sabbaths ['mia ton sabbaton']**, at our having gathered to break bread . . . for he hurried if it may be possible for him to be in Jerusalem **by the day of Pentecost**' (Acts 20:6-16).

Continuing on from the last chapter, once again all three sample versions have altered 'one of the sabbaths' to 'the first day of the week'.

Only when translated literally, as should be expected, does this text endorse the method of counting the days between the Festival of Unleavened Bread and Pentecost—Sabbath-by-Sabbath—as described in Leviticus 23:15, which is something the redactors have been oblivious to or have completely ignored because it compromises the blanket mistranslation, 'the first day of the week'.

The literal text clearly explains that Paul sailed from Troas after the days of Unleavened Bread (verse 6) and met with brethren on one of the (seventh-day) Sabbaths (verse 7) between Wave Sheaf and Pentecost (verse 16).

It is hard to imagine how it could have been written any more clearly.

The failure to correctly identify this fact has further exposed the systematic replacement of 'one of the sabbaths' with the interpolation 'first day of the week', which has been applied to every instance where it appears throughout the New Testament, including 1 Corinthians 16:2:

CLNT: 'On **one of the sabbaths** let each of you lay aside by himself in store that in which he should be prospered, that no collections may be occurring then, whenever I come.'

This is a further instance where untold generations of sincere believers have been led into this systematic falsification of the texts, which now passes as biblical truth.

An apt description of this process appears in Ephesians 4:13-14:

CLNT: 'Unto the end that we should all attain to the unity of the faith and the realization of the Son of God, to a mature (hu)man . . . that we may by no means be minors, surging hither and thither and being carried about by every wind of teaching, by human caprice, by craftiness with a view to the systematizing of the deception.'

Chapter Nine

Exhibit 9

Counting the days between Passover and Pentecost

Part 2:

The method of identifying the Sabbaths between *Passover and Pentecost* according to Leviticus 23 is also evident in Luke 6:1.

CLNTG

C ΛB B ΛΤШΔЄΥΤЄ POΠ PШΤШΔ [40]
SABBATH   second-BEFORE-most   TO

CLNT: 'Now it occurred on **the second first Sabbath [sabbato deuteroproto]** . . .'

KJV: 'And it came to pass on **the second sabbath after the first** . . .'
NASB: 'Now it came about on **a certain Sabbath** . . .'
RSV: 'On **a Sabbath** . . .'

When compared to the literal translation of this text, it can be seen that the **KJV** has altered its composition to conform to a traditional gentile understanding (as was done previously in Matthew 28:1, Luke

23:54, etc.), thereby giving an ambiguous meaning. It could mean either two Sabbaths after the first Sabbath or the Sabbath next after the first Sabbath. However, the rendition 'second sabbath after the first, does indicate a text that literally read *'second first sabbath'* was being used.

It is possible that the scribe responsible for the manuscript used by the **NASB** may have been uncertain about 'a certain Sabbath', although it does reveal that the source text was referring to *a specific* Sabbath. This version contains the following margin note: 'Many mss read, *the second first Sabbath*, i.e., "the second Sabbath after the first."'

The **RSV** contains the following footnote: 'Other ancient authorities read "On the second first sabbath" (on the second sabbath after the first).'

Just as we have observed earlier with *'a sabbath lighted up'*, some of the sample versions were confused about what this text was actually referring to, as is also evident in the words that followed (Luke 6:1 continued):

CLNT: 'He is going through the sowings, and His disciples plucked the ears and ate.'

KJV: 'That he went through the cornfields; and his disciples plucked the ears of corn and ate.'

NASB: 'He was passing through some grainfields; and His disciples were picking and eating the heads of wheat.'

RSV: 'While he was going through the grainfields, his disciples plucked and ate some ears of grain.'

Luke is identifying the Torah mitzvah (commandment) of gleaning, which in this case occurred on the first seventh-day Sabbath after the waving of the first sheaf of the barley harvest.

CVOT: 'When you reap the harvest of your land, moreover, you shall not reap to the very corners of your field, neither shall you gather the gleaning of your harvest; you are to leave them for the needy and the alien. I am **Yahweh** your Elohim' (Leviticus 23:22).

This 'second first sabbath' ('sabbato deuteroprotos') is identified by Strong's Concordance in relation to Luke 6:1 as follows:

> Deuteroprotos . . . second first, i.e. (spec.) a designation
> of the sabbath immediately after the Paschal week (being
> the second after Passover day, and the first of the seven
> Sabbaths intervening before Pentecost):- second . . . after
> the first. (no. 1207)

The three sample versions acknowledge that the 'second first sabbath' is referring to *a seventh-day Sabbath* and the existence of 'deuteroprotos' in many ancient texts by each offering the same ambiguous explanation, 'the second Sabbath after the first', in either the text or the footnotes.

Considering the fact that we have earlier established that Mark's 'first sabbath' (16:9) has been 'corrected' to 'the first day of the week', one would have thought that the redactors to be consistent should have been obliged to similarly correct Luke's 'second first sabbath' to 'the second first day of the week'!

Fortunately, the absurdity of such a translation has not (yet!) eventuated, and the prosecution and 'the defence' are finally in agreement that these Greek texts are identifying seventh-day Sabbaths.

Luke 6:1 identifies 'the second first sabbath' as the first seventh-day Sabbath following Matthew's *second* 'sabbaton', which, put another way, not only identifies that the 'first sabbath' is one and the same as Matthew's second 'sabbaton', but also that it *must* be a seventh-day Sabbath.

This 'first sabbath' was identified earlier in Leviticus 23:11 (and supported by Mark 16:9), and with Luke's text, we have now identified the second 'sabbaton' in Matthew 28:1 as the first seventh-day Sabbath after the day of Passover, not 'the first day of the week'.

Unless the tentacles of tradition prevent you from doing so, you should now be very much aware that 'mia sabbaton', 'one of the sabbaths', throughout the New Testament refers to seventh-day Sabbaths and never to the illusory interpolation 'the first day of the week'.

You may have difficulty in believing texts such as 'second first sabbath' (or 'a sabbath lighted up') if they do not appear in your Bible(s), so let us examine the inclusion of those texts in 'The Trial'.

Word meanings are resolved by the context in which they are used. It should go without saying that if the context has been misunderstood and/or mistranslated, a word or passage will take on a meaning that was not originally intended.

This becomes even more evident where words have been either omitted or added to support the various misinterpretations used to establish the current doctrines under scrutiny.

Harper's Bible Dictionary notes the following (abbreviated):

> The science of textual criticism began when scholars became aware of the multitude of variant readings in the MSS of the Greek New Testament . . . Every reading has to be weighed and considered on its own merits. This is sometimes called the 'eclectic' method. Readings supported by ancient witnesses, especially when these come from a wide geographical area, are generally preferred. The quality, not the quantity, of MSS is the determining factor in choosing a reading. Also, the shorter reading is usually preferred, for scribes tended to add or expand. Moreover, the more difficult reading is usually correct, since copyists tended to ease difficult readings. In parallel texts . . . differences in readings are generally preferred, for there was a tendency to harmonise parallel passages.' (pages 1052-1053, Harper & Row, Publishers)

Unless a scribe engaged in the task of accurately translating a source document was under an instruction that required a particular text to be interpreted to support an existing doctrine, which no doubt sometimes occurred, he would present the text as accurately as possible to reflect the originally intended meaning.

If the source texts contained 'deuteroprotos', it would logically indicate a customary meaning regardless of how obscure it may have appeared to be; therefore, a scribe focused upon conveying the literal meaning would be obliged to translate it as '*the second first Sabbath*', which the three versions being compared with the literal version of events acknowledge by identifying that it appears in many ancient texts.

It is illogical to believe that a scribe would insert the words 'deutero-protos' ('second first') because it would have made no sense to anyone who read it.

For this reading to have survived in many ancient manuscripts, it indicates that the meaning of 'the second first sabbath' was well understood and underlines the necessity of consistently translating such texts literally. Unfortunately, it later fell victim to the systematic pattern of doctrinal correction so evident throughout 'The Trial'.

It also illustrates the importance of using the Jewish calendar and how it enables us to accurately identify the period between Passover and Pentecost in both the Old and New Testaments as it was understood by Moses, Matthew, Mark, Luke, John, and Paul.

Consequently, according to the scriptural principle of 'a little here, a little there', its association with 'the first sabbath' in Leviticus 23:11, 15 and Mark 16:2, 9,* is now obvious.

* Although all three sample versions include verses 9-20, of the three codices used in this study, it appears only in the codex Alexandrinus.

It is interesting to note that there has obviously been some editorial alteration of Mark 16:9 in the other two codices used in 'The Trial',

as the astute observation of A. E. Knoch, principal translator of the
Concordant Literal publications used throughout 'The Trial', reveals:

> B (&) *S* (Vaticanus and Sinaiticus) omit all from 'up-
> standing' ('rising') to the end, but B admits a longer
> conclusion by leaving a blank column for it and *S* spaces
> out the text of the last few pages, which were written in a
> different hand.

This same issue (of difficult readings) has arisen with the reference
to 'light' ('phos') in Luke 23:54 ('epi***phos***ken', 'lighted up'), where in
spite of its appearance in all three codices the three sample versions
have chosen to omit it.

Because of this, Christians are now generally unaware that the texts
refer to the customary practice of lighting up lamps before Sabbaths in
those days, another step leading to the commonly held but mistaken
belief that the New Testament was written primarily for Gentiles.

It should now be clearly understood that these readings reveal that

a) Luke's 'lighted up' occurred at the end of the day of Passover
   before the festival Sabbath had begun;
b) Matthew's use of the term 'lighting up' identified the same
   time of the day preceding the seventh day Sabbath;
c) Luke's 'second first sabbath' was a seventh-day Sabbath, which
   as a result identifies that the preceding seventh-day Sabbath
   was *the first* 'first sabbath';

d) following His resurrection, it was in the morning of this first seventh-day Sabbath that Mark 16:9 says **Yaishua** first appeared to Mary Magdalene;

e) the gospels all identify that 'one of the sabbaths' are in agreement with Leviticus 23:11, 15 and Mark 16:1, 9, and that therefore 'one of the sabbaths' is one and the same as 'the first sabbath'.

Like *all* the original Jewish followers of **Yaishua** (Matthew 15:24), you are now able to identify the events and customs the way they were written and understood in the ancient texts without being converted to an illusory Gentile version of them.

Chapter Ten

Exhibit 10

'Three days and three nights' or 'Good Friday to Easter Sunday'?

CLNT: 'For even as Jonah was in the bowel of the sea monster **three days and three nights**, thus will the Son of Man(kind) be in the heart of the earth **three days and three nights**' (Matthew 12:40).

The Greek text is not supplied here and in other places where all bibles translate the texts literally. In spite of the fact that all three sample versions agree with the wording 'three days and three nights', because 'one of the sabbaths' was altered to the spurious 'first day of the week', it was impossible for it to be translated literally as it was intended.

This is another example of where a text has been misconstrued in one passage of scripture ('first day of the week') it causes an adverse impact upon texts elsewhere (Matthew 12:40>28:1).

This has resulted in the contrived meaning of approximately thirty-nine hours—the three hours between the time of **Yaishua's** death at the ninth hour (3 p.m.) and sunset on Friday being counted as the first day, the twenty-four hours from sunset on Friday to sunset on

Saturday counted as the first night and second day, and the twelve hours from sunset on Saturday to dawn on Easter Sunday morning as the second night and third day.

Disregarding for the moment the fact that there are only *two nights* between Friday afternoon and Sunday morning, **Yaishua** also underlined the fact that He meant three days and *three nights* when He said He would be raised '*after three days*'.

CLNT: 'The Son of Man(kind) is being given up into the hands of men and they will be killing Him, and being killed, after three days He will be rising' (Mark 9:31, 8:31, 10:34).

This is the way the chief priests and Pharisees also understood it when they appeared before Pilate.

CLNT: 'Lord we are reminded that that deceiver said while still living: **"After three days shall I be roused."'**

However, if the third day was *a Sunday,* 'after' the third day would result in a Sunday resurrection at about *sunset* at the earliest or, according to the belief that **Yaishua** was resurrected at *dawn* and to achieve a third night, on Monday morning!

30 CE and 33 CE*

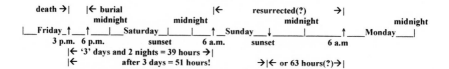

*A problem arises with this 33 CE doctrine, which will be addressed in the next chapter.

The **31** CE concept allows for a literal three days and three nights.

We can now illustrate a simplified form of the restoration of the original jigsaw as follows:

```
 Ninth hour →|   |← sunset
 Yaishua dies →|   |← buried                        resurrected →||← sunset
    |__14 Nisan___|_____15 Nisan_____|___16 Nisan____|____17 Nisan___||___18 Nisan____|
...Monday→|← Tuesday  →|← Wednesday  →|← Thursday →|←  Friday   →|← Saturday...
   midnight         midnight         midnight      midnight      midnight
```

With the fine print added, it looks like this:

32 CE (A)

```
                  dies →|     |← buried                   resurrected →|
  sunset         3 p.m.      |← sunset      sunset        sunset        sunset            sunset
  |___14 Nisan___↑___↑___|___15 Nisan*¹___|__16 Nisan__|_17 Nisan__↑|__18 Nisan*²___|
                           |←   1ˢᵗ day   →|← 2ⁿᵈ day →|← 3ʳᵈ day →|←   Sabbath    →|
  'a Sabbath lighted up' →|  |← fest. Sabbath →|← 'evening of the sabbaths' Matthew 27:66
       Luke 23:54          |← 'in the heart of the earth 3 days & 3 nights' →|
                               approximately 72 hours, Matthew 12:40
                     |← 'and being killed, after 3 days He will be rising'  →|
                                        Mark 9:31
                     |←          'after 3 days shall I be roused'           →|
                     |←      approximately 75 hours Matthew 27:63           →|
```

*¹ **First day of Unleavened Bread, Leviticus 23:6-7.**
*² **'First sabbath' in Mark 16:9; 'one of the sabbaths' in Mathew 28:1, Mark 16:2, Luke 24:1, John 20:1, 19.**

Which with our current method of time-keeping added is:

32 CE (B)

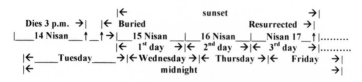

```
                        |←                    sunset              →|
        Dies 3 p.m.  →|   |← Buried                 Resurrected →|
        |___14 Nisan___↑__↑→|___15 Nisan ___|___16 Nisan___|___Nisan 17__↑|.........
                        |←  1ˢᵗ day  →|← 2ⁿᵈ day →|← 3ʳᵈ day →|..........
        |←_____Tuesday_____→|←Wednesday →|← Thursday →|←   Friday   →|
        |←                          midnight                       →|


        |←                           Nisan (sunset to sunset)                →|
        |←    18   →|←    19    →|←20→|← 21 →|← 22 →|← 23 →|← 24 →|←        25      →|
   *¹ →|1ˢᵗ Sabbath*² |Wave Sheaf*³|_____|__*⁴_|_____|_____|_____|_____|2ⁿᵈ first sabbath*⁵|
        |  Saturday  |   Sunday   | Mon | Tues |  Wed  | Thurs |  Fri  |  Saturday    |
        |←                          midnight to midnight                     →|
```

*¹ **Resurrection: 'lighting up into one of the sabbaths' (before Sabbath), Matthew 28:1.**

*² **'First sabbath' (seventh day): Leviticus 23:11, 15 & Mark 16:9 the same day as the 'second sabbaton' in Matthew 28:1.**

*³ **'From the morrow after the first sabbath the priest shall wave it.' (Sunday), Leviticus 23:11.**

*⁴ **Seventh day of Unleavened Bread, 21 Nisan (Tuesday), Leviticus 23:8.**

*⁵ **'Second first sabbath' (seventh day), Luke 6:1.**

Chapter Eleven

Exhibit 11

Up to this point, the prosecution has demonstrated that the current sincerely believed biblical interpretations are unsupported by the fine print of the ancient Greek scriptures.

However, to be credible, the literal fine print found in the scriptures presented herein must also be astronomically and historically accurate; therefore, the question of how the evidence presented thus far fits with those two sciences must now be established.

Astronomical Calculations
United States Naval Observatory calculation of 14 Nisan (Passover) full moon:

28 CE	29 CE	30 CE	31 CE	32 CE	33 CE
Mon.	Sun.	Thurs.	Tues.	Mon.	Fri.
29 Mar.	17 Apr.	6 Apr.	27 Mar.	14 Apr.	3 Apr.

From the above calculations, because **Yaishua** died at about the ninth hour (approximately 3 p.m.) *following the night of the appearance of the* *full moon*, it means His death would have occurred in the following years as indicated below:

33 CE: **3 p.m. on** *Saturday*, **4 April.**
32 CE: **3 p.m. on** *Tuesday*, **15 April.**
31 CE: **3 p.m. on** *Wednesday*, **28 March.**
30 CE: **3 p.m. on** *Friday*, **7 April.**
29 CE: 3 p.m. on *Sunday*, **17 April.**
28 CE: 3 p.m. on *Monday*, **29 March.**

These calculations are very revealing for the following reasons:

i) Because Passover **began** on a Friday at sunset in 33 CE, the crucifixion would have taken place on a **Saturday** and not on 'Good Friday'.

ii) Because it is traditionally claimed that the resurrection took place on Easter Sunday morning and since according to the above calculation the crucifixion took place on Saturday, it means that **Yaishua** would have been resurrected fifteen hours after He died. No matter how you attempt to manipulate the figures, it is impossible for three hours of one day (3 p.m. to sunset) and one night (sunset to dawn) to be 'three days and three nights'!

iii) The *31* CE doctrine correctly believes that the above astronomical calculations support the claim that theoretically permitted a Wednesday crucifixion. However, for reasons explained earlier, this is the only aspect that is in harmony with the scriptural texts.

iv) In **30 CE** Passover began on a Thursday at sunset, which would result in a Friday crucifixion and only *two nights* from the time of burial to the time of the supposed resurrection.

On the other hand the prosecution has revealed that 'one of the sabbaths' was a seventh-day Sabbath and that the women came to the tomb as the Sabbath was lighted up immediately before the day began at sunset late on **Friday**.

Counting back from the time **Yaishua** said He would be 'in the heart of the earth' for three days and three nights (about seventy-two hours), this would have resulted in the crucifixion occurring on a **Tuesday**.

The above astronomical calculations reveal that the only year this was possible was in **32 CE**.*

* It is interesting to note that Sir Robert Anderson calculated from Daniel 9:25-26 that the crucifixion took place at the time of Passover in 32 CE.

When tested by the evidence submitted throughout 'The Trial', the three traditional doctrines fail on practically all counts and should fail to satisfy even the most biased of judges, whereas the substance of the prosecution's case has been sustained by each and every evidential test.

Chapter Twelve

Exhibit 12

Historical issues

CLNT: 'Now **in the fifteenth year of the government of Tiberius Caesar** . . . came a declaration of God to John, the son of Zechariah' (Luke 3:1-2).

The facts are that Tiberius's predecessor, Octavian (Caesar Augustus), died on **19 August 14** CE. Obviously, he ceased to govern at that time(!).

Josephus* states that Tiberius reigned for *twenty-two years, five months, and three days.*

* Jewish Antiquities 18.6.10 (All quotations of Josephus are taken from The New Complete Works of Josephus, translated by William Whiston, commentary by Paul L. Maier. Published by Kregel Publications, P.O. Box 2607, Grand Rapids, MI 59501).

Historians are generally agreed that Tiberius died on **16 March 37** CE and date the succession of Roman emperors following Tiberius's death from this day, beginning with Caligula (Gaius) in *37 CE* (which coincidentally was the year of Josephus's birth).

Therefore, by deducting Josephus's twenty-two years, five months, and three days from 16 March 37 CE, we can ascertain that Tiberius began to govern as emperor in 14 CE.

According to Josephus, that would have been about the middle of October* in *14 CE*, whereas the prosecution asserts that Tiberius began to govern as emperor on 17 September, which is believed to be the date the Roman Senate enrolled Augustus among the gods of the Roman State. Others believe that he began to govern from the time of Augustus's death on 19 August *14 CE*.

* From this it is clear that Josephus reckoned the years of the reign of Tiberius from the anniversary of his accession to the principate, unlike Luke who reckoned it according to the Jewish Calendar.

The Encyclopaedia Britannica* states that following the death of Augustus, 'Tiberius, now supreme, played politics with the Senate and did not allow it to name him emperor for almost a month, but on September 17 he succeeded to the principate. He was 56 years old.'

*Encyclopaedia Britannica, 15th edition, volume 18, page 370. Published on behalf of Encyclopaedia Britannica, Inc.

By reckoning Tiberius's first year from the time he became emperor until the last day of Adar and each successive year from 1 Nisan, it can be determined that, according to Luke, the fifteenth year of Tiberius's government began on 1 Nisan in *28 CE*.

```
         |←                          1 Nisan                        →|
    14 CE  15   16   17   18   19   20   21   22   23   24   25   26   27   28         29
    |_1st year_|_2nd_|_3rd_|_4th_|_5th_|_6th_|_7th_|_8th_|_9th_|_10th_|_11th_|_12th_|_13th_|_14th_|____15th____|
    |← 17 September 14 CE
```

Leaving aside the weight of evidence proving that *'the first day of the week'* doctrine is now discredited, it can now be stated without any shadow of doubt that *the doctrinal assertions that Yaishua died in either 30 CE or 31 CE, both of which rely on the claim that Tiberius began to reign earlier than 14 CE, are untenable.*

This is brought into even clearer focus when we add twenty-two years, five months, and three days to 12 CE, we find Tiberius would have died in **35 CE**, which is not only contrary to the overwhelming view of historians but also impacts upon the dating of the beginning of the reigns of successive emperors following the death of Tiberius.

Let us compare these beliefs to see if they agree with the evidence presented thus far based upon the implication of a generally believed *AD 12* beginning of Tiberius's governance as emperor.

30 CE:

```
        |←                            Nisan                          →|
   12     13     14     15     16     17     18     19     20     21     22     23     24     25     26     27
   |  1st  |  2nd  |  3rd  |  4th  |  5th  |  6th  |  7th  |  8th  |  9th  |  10th  |  11th  |  12th  |  13th  |  14th  |  15th  |
                                           fifteenth year of Tiberius 26–27 CE →|
                                           John commissioned sometime in 26 CE →|
```

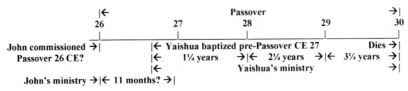

```
                  |←                        Passover                     →|
                  26                  27                  28                  29                  30
        _____|_____|_____|_____|_____|
   John commissioned →|            |← Yaishua baptized pre-Passover CE 27          Dies →|
   Passover 26 CE?                  |←        1¼ years      →|←     2¼ years     →|← 3¼ years  →|
                                    |←              Yaishua's ministry                        →|
   John's ministry →|← 11 months? →|
```

31 CE:

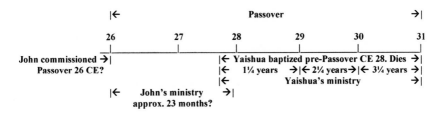

33 CE

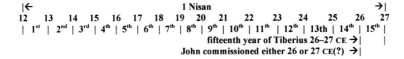

If these were true, it would mean:

i) because it is claimed that the first year of Tiberius's government began in 12 CE, his fifteenth year began 1 Nisan in 26 CE and ended in Adar 27 CE.

ii) if that were the case, by adding the length of Tiberius's tenure as Caesar, twenty-two plus years according to Josephus, Tiberius would have died in *35 CE*.

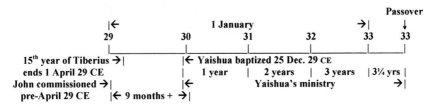

This raises the problem that if John was commissioned in late June 29 CE, six months before it is believed **Yaishua** turned 30 on the 25 December, it would have been after Tiberius's fifteenth year had ended (his sixteenth year began at the beginning of April 29 CE).

In that case, if **Yaishua** turned 30 on 25 December and John was commissioned prior to April, John would have been at least nine months older, rather than approximately six months as identified by the scripture (Luke 1:24-56). This means John would not have yet become 30 when he was commissioned.

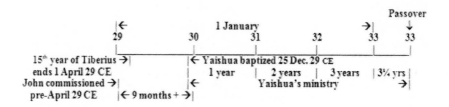

Tiberius

In 6 BCE, Tiberius was granted the powers of a tribune, one of the highest Roman offices and is an office Augustus also held. However, he abdicated that position by going into voluntary exile, incurring the wrath of Augustus, and he was unable to return to Rome for almost ten years as a result.

Tiberius regained all of his former powers by 4 CE, the year in which the second of Augustus' grandsons, Gaius, who had been groomed to succeed him died in 4 CE (the other, Lucius, died in 2 CE), leaving Augustus little choice but to choose Tiberius as his successor.

In *13 CE*,* Augustus's powers were extended by the Senate for a further ten years, and Tiberius, by now the only logical candidate to succeed him, was given sweeping constitutional powers.

* Encyclopaedia Britannica, 15th edition.

Tiberius himself left Rome in 27 CE, never to return, and granted similar authority as he had under Octavian to the head of the praetorian guard, Lucius Aurelius Sejanus soon became the most powerful figure in Rome, with Tiberius being now seen merely as a figurehead.

By 31 CE, Tiberius realized that the extent of Sejanus's powers threatened his own position, and he sent orders to the Senate to have him summarily executed, which was carried out expeditiously.

Although Sejanus had powers and influence similar to those that Tiberius himself had before Octavian's death, nowhere does he appear in the historical record as governing as emperor and neither would have Tiberius had he pre-deceased Augustus. Clearly, Luke's first year of the government of Tiberius Caesar was not based upon a 12 CE date.

Chapter Thirteen

Exhibit 13

The calendar

CVOT: 'This month shall be for you the beginning of months. It shall be the first for you of the months of the year' (Exodus 12:2).

For the purposes of this study, we are primarily concerned with the timing of the festivals. It is clear that the scriptures we have examined (unsurprisingly) all reflect a strong Jewish description of the events, unlike the contrived 'first day of the week' doctrine.

Evidence of this has been revealed by the failure to understand and/or include any reference to 'one of the Sabbaths' in the Gospel resurrection accounts, nor 'lighting/lighted up' before Sabbath days, nor the counting of the Sabbaths between the days of Unleavened Bread and Pentecost beginning with the second first Sabbath, etc.

These systematic alterations have purged the 'Jewishness' from the Greek scriptures regarding the death and resurrection accounts, which has played a large part in forming the various opinions surrounding which calendar was used.

The time of these events, Passover, the days of Unleavened Bread, and the sacrificial nature of **Yaishua's** death as 'the Lamb of God Which takes away the sins of the world' (John 1:29), play a central part in the scriptural narrative; consequently, it is necessary to use the calendar used in Israel during the time of these events.

Both Luke's Gospel and the Acts of the Apostles are addressed to Theophilus, leading to the belief that Luke was the author of both accounts.

Very little is known about Theophilus, although it is obvious he was a fellow Christian who was believed to be a Gentile. As a consequence, it is generally claimed that Luke, an associate of Paul during his travels, wrote using a calendar specifically used and/or understood by Theophilus.

This is not consistent with the fact that Luke's Gospel and the Acts of the Apostles make extensive references to Jewish customs and practices; therefore, it would have been necessary for Theophilus to have understood Luke's (and Paul's) writings according to the Jewish calendar.

The prosecution has revealed that this is an important feature in understanding the entire New Testament, although it has been well concealed in the 'defendant' Bible versions used in 'The Trial'.

Another feature is Luke's frequent references to Paul teaching in synagogues throughout his travels.

CLNT: 'Now he came to be with the disciples in Damascus some days. And immediately in the synagogues he heralded Jesus, that He is the Son of God . . . Now as a considerable number of days were fulfilled the Jews consult to assassinate him' (Acts 9:19-25).

CLNT: 'And coming to be in Salamis they (Paul and Silas) announced the word in the synagogues of the Jews . . . Now they . . . came along into Antioch, Pisidia, and entering into the synagogue on the day of the sabbaths . . . they are seated. Now after the reading of the Law and the Prophets the chief of the synagogue dispatch to them saying: "Men, brethren, if there be any word of entreaty for the people, say it" . . . Now the synagogue having broken up, many of the Jews and reverent proselytes follow Paul and Barnabas, who, speaking to them, persuaded them to remain in the grace of God . . . Now on the coming sabbath almost the entire city was gathered to hear the word of the Lord' (Acts 13:5, 14, 43-44).

'Almost the entire city' implies that Jews, proselytes, and Gentile Christians (at least) gathered on the Sabbath to hear Paul. This hardly suggests that these were followers of a 'first day of the week' doctrine.

CLNT: 'Both Paul and Silas . . . (were) coming along into the synagogue of the Jews . . . who receive the word with all eagerness, examining the Scriptures day by day to see if these have it thus. Many of them, indeed, then believe and of the respectable Greek women and men not a few' (Acts 17:10-12).

CLNT: 'Now he argued in the synagogue on every sabbath and persuaded both Jews and Greeks' (Acts 18:4).

CLNT: 'Now entering the synagogue he spoke boldly for three months, arguing and persuading as to that which concerns the kingdom of God . . . Now as some were hardened and stubborn, saying evil things of the way before the multitude, withdrawing from them he severs the disciples, arguing day by day in the school of Tyrannus. Now this occurred for two years, so that all those dwelling in the province of Asia hear the word of the Lord (Greek 'Kyrios'), both Jews and Greeks' (Acts 19:8).

From these texts, it is clear that Paul openly and frequently preached in the synagogues on Sabbath days. On the other hand, there is no scriptural evidence that he fellowshipped with Christian brethren on the first day of the week, let alone as a weekly 'Sabbath'.

The proselytes present in the synagogues would have been instructed by the rabbis according to the Hebrew texts and customs in conjunction with the Jewish calendar in the same way the New Testament authors referred to them, including Luke.

You should be aware by now that without becoming acquainted with the meaning of various Jewish customs that frequently appear in the scriptural texts, which were dependent upon the Jewish calendar, it is not possible to have an accurate comprehension of these authors' intended meanings, e.g. lighting up into Sabbaths.

As we can see from Luke's writings, Theophilus was well-informed regarding these issues.

Paul, Luke's mentor, did not attempt to convert Gentiles to a 'first day of the week sabbath' replacement theology, nor would he have hypocritically altered his seventh-day Sabbath observance to a yet to be devised 'first day of the week' version of events when teaching

Gentiles while openly fellowshipping with both Jews and Gentiles on the seventh-day Sabbath.

There is a name for this; it is called hypocrisy, something that Paul was very particular not to engage in.

Chapter Fourteen

Exhibit 14

The commissioning of John the Baptist

CLNT: 'Now in those days coming along is John . . . Then went out to him Jerusalem and entire Judea and the entire country about the Jordan' (Matthew 3:1-15).

CLNT: 'John the Baptist came to be in the wilderness and is heralding a baptism of repentance for the pardon of sins and out to him went the entire province of Judea and all the Jerusalemites' (Mark 1:4).

CLNT: 'And he [John] came into the entire country about the Jordan . . . Indeed entreating about many things also he brought the evangel to the people' (Luke 3:1).

From these passages, we can establish that John travelled extensively and that he 'entreated about many things', so he did more than simply immerse people in the river Jordan.

We also need to take into account that, as well as the likelihood that he began his priestly Temple duties at the time of the major festivals when the population was greatly increased, John would have ministered to and baptised many of the visiting pilgrims.

Josephus* states that during the siege of Jerusalem at the time of the destruction of the Temple in 70 CE, about forty years after John was commissioned, between 2.565-3 million people were gathered in Jerusalem for Passover.

* The New Complete works of Josephus. Revised and expanded edition. The Jewish War, book 6, chapter 9 (note 3).

Before we continue this inquiry, it will be helpful to try and establish approximately when John baptized **Yaishua**.

Chapter Fifteen

Exhibit 15

Yaishua's baptism

CLNT: 'And He, Jesus, when beginning was **about thirty years old**' (Luke 3:23).

This is generally interpreted to mean that **Yaishua** had turned 30 but had not yet reached the age of 31; in other words, He was in His thirty-first year.

Let us examine the above text in the way we confirmed the consistent literal meaning of 'opse' in Matthew 28:1 to see how the same word translated as 'about'* was used elsewhere in relation to numbers.

*Strong's no. 5616: 'Hosei.'

CLNT: 'Now Miriam remains with her **about** three months' (Luke 1:56).

CLNT: 'For there were **about** five thousand men . . . Now it occurred **about** eight days after these sayings' (Luke 9:14, 28).

CLNT: 'And He is pulled away from them **about** a stone's throw . . . and after an interval of **about** one hour' (Luke 22:41, 59).

CLNT: 'And it was already **about** the sixth hour' (Luke 23:44).

Luke's gospel also uses the Greek word 'hosper' (*Strong's* no. 5613).

CLNT: 'For he had a daughter **about** 12 years old' (Luke 8:42).

It can readily be seen that each is a generalization and, according to the author, not a precise figure.

NB: The prosecution is not saying that it is impossible for such to be an exact number but that the author was not certain of the exact figure.

Matthew reveals a clear difference between when a number is precise and when it is intended to be an approximation:

CLNT: 'And they pick up of the superfluous fragments, **twelve panniers** full. Now those eating were **about (hosei) five thousand** men' (Matthew 14:20-21).

Matthew was certain that there were exactly twelve panniers but uncertain about the actual number of men.

The prosecution states that Luke intended to convey the same sense of generality (Luke chapter 3:23); had he not intended to do so, he would not have used 'hosei'. Neither does the text say that **Yaishua** was baptised when He 'became' 30 or six months after John was commissioned, which are common presumptions. These will be dealt with in a later chapter.

CLNT: 'The beginning of the evangel of Jesus Christ, Son of God . . . and it occurred in those days that Jesus came from Nazareth of Galilee and is baptized in the Jordan by John . . . and **straightway** the spirit is ejecting Him into the wilderness. And He was in the wilderness **forty days** . . . Now after the giving up of John, Jesus came into Galilee' (Mark 1:1-13).

CLNT: 'Now it occurred that as all the people are baptized, at Jesus also being baptized' (Luke 3:21).

CLNT: 'At that season Herod the tetrarch hears tidings of Jesus and said to his pages: "This is John the Baptist. He was roused from the dead and therefore powerful deeds are operating in him." For Herod then, holding John, binds him and puts him in jail . . . and sending, he beheads John in the jail' (Matthew 14:1-12).

It should be noted that **Yaishua** was baptized in the latter part of John's ministry and that John was imprisoned shortly after and subsequently beheaded.

From John 1:28-43 and John 2:1, 12-13, we can deduce that **Yaishua's** baptism took place not long before a Passover festival.

CLNT: 'These things occurred in Bethany, the other side of the Jordan river, where John was baptizing. On the morrow he is observing

Jesus coming toward him, and is saying: "Lo! The Lamb of God Which is taking away the sin of the world! This is He concerning Whom I said, 'After me is coming a Man Who has come to be in front of me, for He was First, before me.' And I was not aware of Him. But that He may be manifested to Israel, therefore came I, baptizing in water." And John testifies, saying that "I have gazed upon the spirit, descending as a dove out of heaven, and it remains on Him. And I was not aware of Him, but He Who sends me to be baptizing in water, That One said to me, 'On Whomever you may be perceiving the spirit descending and remaining on Him, This is He Who is baptizing in holy spirit.' And I have seen and have testified that This One is the Son of God." On the morrow John again stood and two of his disciples. And looking at Jesus walking, he is saying: "Lo! The Lamb of God!" And the two disciples hear him speaking and they follow Jesus . . . On the morrow He wants to come away into Galilee and is finding Philip and Jesus is saying: "Follow Me." . . . [2:1] And on the third day a wedding occurred in Cana of Galilee . . . [v. 12] After this He descended into Capernaum, He and His mother and His brothers and disciples and they remained there not many days. And near was the Passover of the Jews and Jesus went up into Jerusalem.'

From these accounts, we can readily identify that immediately following His baptism ('straightway'), He spent forty days and forty nights in the wilderness (Mark 1:12, Matthew 4:1, Luke 4:2).

On His return, some disciples joined Him, and very soon after, He, His family, and His disciples attended a wedding at Cana in Galilee, following which they travelled to Capernaum, where they stayed 'for not many days'. Because Passover was near, He then travelled to Jerusalem for Passover (John 1:29-2:13).

As a result, we can determine that **Yaishua** was baptized approximately two months before the Passover festival.

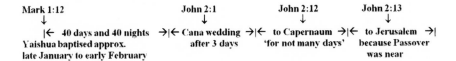

Mark 1:12	John 2:1	John 2:12	John 2:13
↓	↓	↓	↓
|← 40 days and 40 nights →|←	Cana wedding →|←	to Capernaum →|←	to Jerusalem →|
Yaishua baptised approx. late January to early February	after 3 days	'for not many days'	because Passover was near

Chapter Sixteen

Exhibit 16

Yaishua's ministry

We have earlier established that **Yaishua** died at the time of Passover in *32 CE* (15 April). If we can determine how many Passovers He attended from the time He was baptized until His death and deduct them from **32 CE**, we will know approximately how long His ministry was, when He was baptized, and the approximate length of John's ministry.

The traditional doctrines are all based on the belief that John identified four Passovers, which supposedly appear in John 2:13, 5:1, 6:4, and 11:55.

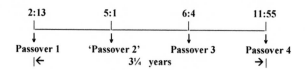

However, John's Gospel specifically identifies only *three* Passovers following **Yaishua's** baptism. When examining John 5:1, where John does not refer to a Passover but *'a festival of the Jews'*, it is noticeable in the previous verse (John 4:54) that:

CLNT: 'Now this, again, is the second sign Jesus does, coming out of Judea into Galilee.'

This is the second sign after the Passover in the year of His baptism. If the very next verse (John 5:1) was the next Passover John omitted almost one year of **Yaishua's** ministry. The prosecution asserts that John did not specifically identify 'the festival of the Jews' as a Passover because it wasn't a Passover.

The arbitrary insertion of John 5:1 has had the same effect as we previously encountered with Matthew 28:1, with the result that translators have been influenced by the traditional doctrinal understanding of Robert Estienne (who is credited with these insertions).

Because 'The Trial' is predicated upon consistently translating all texts literally, we can establish that they literally reveal that **Yaishua** attended only three Passovers from the time of His baptism until His death.

By deducting *two Passovers* from His third and final Passover in *32 CE*, it can now be established that the *first* of these was *30 CE and the year of Yaishua's baptism.*

Allowing for **Yaishua's** forty days in the wilderness, His later visits to Cana and Capernaum, and His travel to Jerusalem for Passover, we can also identify that He was baptized approximately two months before Passover in 30 CE.

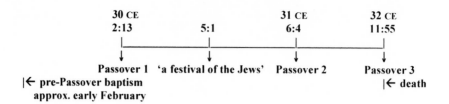

Consequently, the time from His baptism to His death was a period of approximately two years and two months.*

* Some of the early church fathers also believed in an approximate two-year ministry; at least one of them is understood to have believed in a Tuesday crucifixion.

Chapter Seventeen

Summing Up

Yaishua was wont to say: 'It is written.'

The prosecution has revealed to you that 'one of the sabbaths', 'the first sabbath', and 'the second first sabbath' are all written in the fine print of the scriptures. If in fact **Yaishua** quoted from the Septuagint, as many claim, He would have certainly read Leviticus 23:11, 15 as 'the first sabbath'.

'The first day of the week' is *not* written anywhere in the New Testament texts. It is and always has been merely a doctrinal insertion.

The prosecution has identified the clear link between Leviticus 23:11, 15 and the second 'sabbaton' in Matthew 28:1.

His disciples, including Paul, wrote clearly about these issues, which are supported by the literal translations of the fine print as revealed in 'The Trial'.

In studying this question, the prosecution has established beyond any reasonable doubt that:

i)   The word 'sabbaton' appears twice in the ancient Greek texts of Matthew 28:1.

ii)   Each of the sample versions have correctly translated the first 'sabbaton' as 'sabbath' but have misunderstood what day it applied to.

iii) This has resulted in each of the sample versions erroneously correcting the second 'sabbaton' to 'week'.

iv)   The chapters, verses, and punctuation currently employed in most bibles do not exist in the ancient uncial Greek texts. Consequently, when the arbitrarily inserted 'Matthew 28:1' is removed and Matthew's first 'sabbaton' is read in conjunction with the preceding verse, it completely changes the context of the narrative as it is understood by each of the traditional doctrines at this time, rendering each doctrine and all biblical references to 'the first day of the week' redundant.

v)   It has been revealed that this first 'sabbaton' was the festival Sabbath of 15 Nisan, the day the chief priests and Pharisees were authorized by Pilate to seal the tomb.

vi)   The second 'sabbaton' was the seventh-day Sabbath of 18 Nisan. It was in the evening of the day preceding the second 'sabbaton' that, according to Matthew, the women came to view the tomb, only to find that the resurrection had already taken place.

vii) Matthew revealed that this was at the time of 'lighting up into one of the sabbaths'.

viii)   All three traditional doctrines under examination—*30 CE,
        31 CE, and 33 CE*—stand or fall on the question of whether
        or not Matthew's second 'sabbaton' means 'sabbath' or '(the
        first day of) the week'.

ix)   There was a lapse of two nights and two days between the
        two scriptural references to 'sabbaton' in 'Matthew 28:1' and
        therefore three days and three nights (Matthew 12:40) from
        the time of **Yaishua's** burial to His resurrection.

```
    14 Nisan           15 Nisan         16 Nisan    17 Nisan         18 Nisan
|___Passover____|____first sabbaton____|_____|_____|__second sabbaton ___|
  a Sabbath  →|   evening of Sabbaths→|        lighting up into →|
  lighted up                                    one of Sabbaths
              |←  Festival Sabbath  →|←   2 days & 2 nights  →|←  First Sabbath   →|
    Burial →|←                 3 days and 3 nights             →|← Resurrection
```

x)   The first seventh-day Sabbath after Passover, which appears
        as 'one of the sabbaths' in all the ancient Greek Gospel
        accounts, is the day preceding Wave Sheaf, which is
        consistent with Leviticus 23:11.

xi)   Mark 16 also refers to the same day as 'the first sabbath'
        (verse 9).

Since this is the same day as the second 'sabbaton' in Matthew's
account, all references to 'mia(n) sabbaton' ('one of the sabbaths')
throughout the Gospels are to the first seventh-day Sabbath after
Passover, an endorsement of Leviticus 23:11, 15.

Consequently, from Mark 16:9, 'Now rising, in the morning of the
first sabbath', it should be obvious that the resurrection had taken
place before either Sunday morning or Saturday afternoon.

'Rising' is written in the aorist tense, describing an event (rising) that had taken place previously, at the time of lighting up *into* the first sabbath.

xii) Luke 6:1 refers to 'the second first sabbath'. All versions, regardless of how they render this passage, understand this text to be referring to a seventh-day Sabbath. Although the **KJV** interprets this text in an ambiguous way, it is obvious that the source text used in this version contained 'the second first sabbath'. Both the **NASB** and **RSV** contain margin notes indicating their awareness that it appears in many ancient Greek manuscripts but opted to use a text that contained a reading that they considered to be less obscure: 'a certain Sabbath' (NASB) or simply 'a sabbath' (RSV).

xiii) Strong's Concordance (no. 4521) identifies this day as the second seventh-day Sabbath after the day of Passover and is therefore the first of the seven seventh-day Sabbaths between Wave Sheaf and Pentecost.

32 CE:

|Passover |...|← 1st 7th day sabbath → |← Wave Sheaf → |...|← 2nd first sabbath→ |...7 sabbaths + 1 day
|14 Nisan |...|← 18 Nisan → |← 19 Nisan → |...|← 25 Nisan →	9 Sivan →	
14-15 April 17-18 April 18-19 April 24-25 April 6-7 June →	
Mon-Tues   Fri-Sat   Sat-Sun   Fri-Sat   Sat-Sun
Pentecost →	

xiv) If 'the second first sabbath' is a seventh-day Sabbath, then the first 'first sabbath' must also be a seventh-day Sabbath.

xv) This first 'first sabbath' is the same day as the '(first) sabbath' in Leviticus 23:11 and Mark 16:9 and is the same day as the second 'sabbaton' in Matthew 28:1 as well as 'one of the sabbaths' in Mark 16:2, Luke 24:1, and John 20:1, 19.

xvi) Luke 23:54 identifies the time the burial of **Yaishua's** body was completed as 'a sabbath lighted up'. Although the three codices used in 'The Trial' contain this reading, none of the sample Bible versions include it.

As a result, the true context of this reading and its connection to Matthew's reference to 'lighting up into one of the sabbaths' is now unrecognized, which emphasizes the importance of retaining the literal meaning of the fine print in each of these instances.

xvii) **Yaishua** purposefully stated that He would be in the heart of the earth for three days and three nights.

xviii) To underline the fact that He meant a literal three days and three nights, He explained that He would be raised 'after three days' (Mark 8:31, 9:31, and 10:34), which is the way the chief priests and Pharisees understood it when they appeared before Pilate the day after **Yaishua's** assassination (Matthew 27:63).

xix) It has been established that when Matthew identified the time the women came to view the tomb and were told that **Yaishua** was already risen, it was before sunset on Friday, at the time referred to as the 'lighting up into one of the sabbaths'.

This is consistent with the fact that because **Yaishua** was buried immediately before sunset on the day preceding the festival Sabbath and was entombed for three days and three nights as He said he would be, He must have been resurrected at a similar time to that of His burial three days and three nights later, late in the afternoon before sunset and not the next morning.

xx)   This reveals that **Yaishua** died on a Tuesday, three days and three nights prior to the lighting up into one of the Sabbaths.

xxi)   Astronomical calculations establish that *32 CE* was the only year in which this was possible.

xxii)   Astronomical calculations also reveal that in *33 CE* (a year it is claimed the crucifixion took place on Good Friday), Passover, 14 Nisan, *began* on a Friday, which means that the crucifixion would have taken place the following day on the Sabbath, not on 'Good Friday' as claimed.

This in turn means that a 'first day of the week' resurrection is impossible regardless of how the 'three days and three nights' is construed because they cannot be reconfigured to consist of only fifteen hours and one night.

xxiii) Astronomical calculations reveal that in *30 CE*, Passover began on a Thursday, which would require a Friday crucifixion, and a Sunday morning resurrection 'three days' and two nights later.

xxiv) Both the *30 CE* and *31 CE* doctrines rely on the claim that Tiberius began to govern in *12 CE,* contradicting the historical record that he clearly did not.

Regardless of any other evidence, both of these doctrines fail on this point alone and cannot possibly be true.

xxv)   All three doctrines—*30 CE*, *31 CE*, and *33 CE*—fail the test of legitimacy when compared with the literal translations of the ancient Greek texts and/or historical facts and astronomical calculations.

Whereas, the prosecution has proven beyond reasonable doubt that:

a) **Yaishua** died on a Tuesday, 15 April *32 CE*.

b) He was buried immediately prior to sunset on Tuesday at the time the festival Sabbath was 'lighted up'.

c) Astronomical calculation confirms that *32 CE* was the only year in which this could have taken place.

d) Three days and three nights (about seventy-two hours) after **Yaishua's** burial, the women came to the tomb late on Friday, 17 Nisan, at the time of 'lighting up into one of the sabbaths' (before sunset) and were informed that He was already risen from the dead (Matthew 12:40 and 28:1).

e) This Sabbath was the first seventh-day Sabbath after Passover, 18 Nisan, an endorsement of Leviticus 23:11, Mark 16:9, and by implication, Luke 6:1.

f) Tiberius Caesar died in *37 CE* after governing for about twenty-two and a half years, which means that he began to govern in 14 CE.

g) John the Baptist's ministry began in the fifteenth year of the government of Tiberius Caesar, which began on 1 Nisan 28 CE (Luke 3:1-2).

h) According to the literal fine print **Yaishua's** ministry was a little over two years long (John 2:13, 6:4, and 11:55).

i) **Yaishua** was approximately 31 years and 5 months old when He was baptised or, in Luke's words, 'about thirty' and approximately 33 years and 7 months old when He died (Luke 3:21-23).

Chapter Eighteen

The year of Yaishua's birth

From the literal translation of the scriptural texts and the astronomical calculations and historical evidence submitted throughout 'The Trial', it has been clearly established that the Son of God died on Tuesday, 15 April **32** CE.

As a result, it is now possible to identify the year and month of His birth (which is as much in dispute as the orthodox beliefs regarding His death and resurrection) based upon the following:

i)   Because He died in April of **32** CE, we can, by deducting His age from that date, identify that He was born sometime in ***September*** (in the month of Tishri) **3** BCE and that John was born about six months earlier about the time of ***Passover*** in that year.

ii) Tishri is a significant month in the Jewish calendar because three important feasts occurred in that month: Yom Teruah (the Feast of Trumpets, also called Rosh Hashana, the beginning of the civil year) on the first day, Yom Kippur (the Day of Atonement) on the tenth day of Tishri, and Sukkot (the Feast of Tabernacles) beginning on the fifteenth day of the month.

iii) The month in which Passover occurred, Aviv (later called 'Nisan'), is referred to as 'the beginning of months'. 'It shall be first for you of the months of the year' (Exodus 12:2). The dates of the various festivals that are celebrated throughout the year are dated from the beginning of this month.

iv) According to the United States Naval Observatory, in *BCE 3* the new moon (1 Nisan) occurred on 16 March. Therefore, by counting the days from 1 Nisan to 1 Tishri (Rosh Hashana/ Yom Teruah), we will find that 1 Tishri began at sunset on 9 September.

v) On the basis that it takes 29 days, 12 hours, 55 minutes, and 53 seconds for the moon to orbit the earth, there would have been an approximate elapsed time of 177¼ days between 1 Nisan and 1 Tishri.

This is evident in the present-day calendar:

Nisan =	30 days
Iyyar =	29 days
Sivan =	30 days
Tammuz =	29 days
Av =	30 days
Elul =	29 days
Total =	177 days

vi) If **Yaishua** was born at the time of one of the festivals in Tishri *BCE 3* and John at the time of Passover in that year, their births would have occurred at 'appointed times' according to the scriptures.

If we deduct the (approximate) seven-month component of **Yaishua's** age at death on 15 April (the time of Passover in 32 CE), we arrive at approximately mid-September.

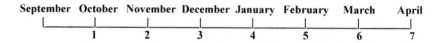

The Festival of Sukkoth (Tabernacles or Booths) began on 24 September and ended on 30 September in 3 CE*.

*It is not known how the calendar was adjusted at that time to accommodate the festivals, as is currently done by the rules of postponement.

This may explain why there was 'no room at the inn' in Bethlehem at the time **Yaishua** was born. Because of its close proximity to Jerusalem it may have been accommodating the overflow of visitors who had arrived for the festival.

It is highly unlikely that Bethlehem would be overcrowded in midwinter nor that people would travel there for the census at that time of the year. In recent times the claim of a 25 December birth doctrine has taken a new twist, which we will examine in the next chapter.

It makes considerably more sense that **Yaishua** was born during one of the scripturally identified appointed times, as has been more than adequately indicated in this study, than to believe that He was born at the time of the death and rebirth of the pagan sun god at the time of the winter solstice, for which there is not one 'iota or serif' (jot or tittle) of scriptural support.

Sept.	Oct.	Nov.	Baptism = approx. Feb. 30 CE* →					
			Dec.	Jan.	Feb.		Mar.	Apr.

|← 3 BCE..30 CE......................32 CE →|
|←   September 3 BCE–14 April 32 CE = 33 years 7 months   →|

The texts relating to the birth of the promised Messiah are briefly examined below.

CLNT: 'Now it occurred in those days that a decree came out from Caesar Augustus that the entire earth register. This first registration occurred when Quirinius is governing Syria. And all went up to register, each into his own city. Now Joseph also went up from Galilee, out of the city of Nazareth, into Judea into the city of David which is called Bethlehem, because of his being of the house and kindred of David, to register together with Miriam, his espoused wife, who is parturient*' (Luke 2:1).

In normal circumstances, if this were in December, both mother and child and those in similar circumstances would be at great risk if giving birth in transit in winter conditions.

***CLNT:** Parturient, 'close to giving birth' or 'great with child' (KJV).

Furthermore, Joseph would surely have taken into consideration the danger, in view of the distance from Nazareth to Bethlehem and the likelihood of the birth occurring during the journey, or alternatively to travel with his family after the birth if it were mid winter.

CLNT: 'Now it came to pass in their being there, the days are fulfilled for her to be bringing forth. And she brings forth her Son, the firstborn, and swaddles Him, and cradles Him in a manger, because there was no place for them in the caravansary . . . And shepherds were in the same district in the field fold, and maintaining watches at night over their flock. And lo! a messenger of the Lord (**YHWH**) stood by them, and the glory of God shines about them, and they were afraid with a great fear' (Luke 2:6-8).

The fact that the shepherds were watching over their flocks day and night in the fields is also a reasonable indicator that **Yaishua** was not born during the winter months. The shepherds would not abandon their flocks during the night but would have waited until daylight when they could safely bring the flocks with them.

CLNT: 'And it occurred, as the messengers came away from them into heaven, that the shepherds spoke to one another, saying, "By all means we may be passing through to Bethlehem . . ." And they came hurrying, and they found both Miriam and Joseph and the Babe lying in the manger' (Luke 2:15-16).

CLNT: 'Now, at Jesus being born in Bethlehem of Judea in the days of Herod the king, lo! magi from the east came along into Jerusalem, saying, "Where is He Who is brought forth King of the Jews? For we perceived His star in the East and we came to worship Him' (Matthew 2:1-2).

It is not stated when the magi arrived in Jerusalem, but they were earlier guided by the star they had perceived 'in the East' after **Yaishua** was born. It is interesting that although they lived in the east, they knew of the promised king of Israel.

This may indicate that they were from Babylon to the east, where references to His coming were provided by Daniel from the time of the Babylonian captivity about 600 years earlier. No doubt Simeon and

Hannah were aware of the imminent coming of the Messiah (Luke 2:25, 36), from texts such as Daniel 9:25, 26.

In any case, it was long enough after the birth that when the magi arrived in Bethlehem, Joseph, Miriam, and **Yaishua** were no longer in a caravansary (in **KJV**, an inn) but were living in a house.

CLNT: 'Now hearing of it, King Herod was disturbed and all Jerusalem with him. And, gathering all the chief priests and scribes of the people, he ascertained from them where the Christ is born. Now they say to him "In Bethlehem of Judea, for thus it is written through the prophet [Micah 5:2]:

CLNT: "And you, Bethlehem, land of Judah,
Are you in any respect least among the mentors of Judah?
For out of you shall come forth the Ruler Who shall shepherd My people Israel."

'Then Herod covertly calling the magi ascertains exactly from them the time of the star's appearing. And sending them to Bethlehem, he said: "Having gone, inquire accurately concerning the little boy. Now, if ever you should be finding Him report to me, so that I also coming should be worshipping Him . . ." and lo! the star which they perceived in the East preceded them till, coming, it was standing over where the little Boy was. Now perceiving the star, they rejoiced with great joy, tremendously. And coming into the house they perceived the little Boy' (Matthew 2:3-11).

Although Herod was disturbed because some foreigners were making inquiries about a recently born king of the Jews whom they wished to worship, his distress would have been even greater to find that *this King's* 'credentials' were clearly greater than his own.

CLNT: 'And being apprised in a trance not to go back to Herod, through another way they retire into their own country.

Now, at their retiring into their country, lo! a messenger of the Lord is appearing in a trance to Joseph, saying, "Being roused, take along the little Boy and His mother and flee into Egypt and be there till I should speak to you, for Herod is about to be seeking the little Boy to destroy Him." Now he, being roused, took along the little Boy and His mother by night and retires into Egypt. And he was there till the decease of Herod . . . Then Herod, perceiving that he was scoffed at by the magi, was very furious and dispatching he massacred all the boys in Bethlehem and in all its boundaries from two years and below, according to the time he ascertains from the magi' (Matthew 2:12-16).

Joseph's instruction to take the little Boy to Egypt occurred after the magi had retired into their own country.

It is possible that this would have taken place some time later, seeing that Herod would not have been immediately aware that the magi were not coming back to report to him about the Child King's whereabouts.

CLNT: 'And when the eight days of His circumcising are fulfilled, His name also was called Jesus, which He was called by the messenger before His conception in the womb. And when the days of their cleansing are fulfilled according to the law of Moses, they brought Him up into Jerusalem to present Him to the Lord*, according as it is written in the law of the Lord*, that every male opening up the matrix shall be called holy to the Lord*, and to give sacrifice according to that which is declared in the law of the Lord*, a pair of turtle doves or two squabs of doves . . . And as they accomplish all according to the law of the Lord,* they return into Galilee, into their own city, Nazareth' (Luke 2:21-24, 39).

* **YHWH.**

The following timeline diagram sets out a suggested approximate time of events:

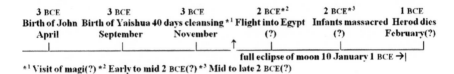

3 BCE	3 BCE	3 BCE	2 BCE*²	2 BCE*³	1 BCE
Birth of John	Birth of Yaishua	40 days cleansing *¹	Flight into Egypt	Infants massacred	Herod dies
April	September	November	(?)	(?)	February(?)

full eclipse of moon 10 January 1 BCE →|

*¹ Visit of magi(?) *² Early to mid 2 BCE(?) *³ Mid to late 2 BCE(?)

If **Yaishua** was born in the month of Tishri **3** BCE, it was before the time in which it is generally believed Herod died (4 BCE).

On what basis is it believed Herod died in 4 BCE?

The reason William Whiston believed so is clearly explained in his translation of the works of Josephus:*

> This eclipse of the moon (which is the only eclipse of either of the luminaries mentioned by our Josephus in any of his writings) **is of the greatest consequence for the determination of the time of the death of Herod and Antipater, and the birth and entire chronology of Jesus Christ.** It occurred on March 13th, in the year of the Julian period 4710, and the 4th year before the Christian era.

* The New Complete Works of Josephus, translated by William Whiston, commentary by Paul L. Maier. Published by Kregel Publications, PO Box 2607, Grand Rapids, MI 49501.

Whiston states that he bases his understanding of the 'entire chronology of Jesus Christ' on his learned opinion of Josephus's mention of an eclipse rather than relying on the scriptures to determine the chronology. The particular eclipse referred to by Whiston was a brief partial eclipse in 4 BCE.

This leaves us with the choice of whether we believe the scriptures are literally accurate or not, the question that lies at the heart of Christian apologetics, and also brings into question the correct year of Herod's death.

The prosecution states that there is no more reliable authority than that which is written in the scriptural texts as they have been literally revealed throughout 'The Trial'.

Had that been the method employed, Josephus's mention of an eclipse would have been better understood as a longer, total eclipse on the 10 January *1 BCE*.

This means that Herod died early in *1 BCE* soon after a total eclipse of the moon.

Accordingly, the evidence presented thus far leads to the conclusion that Whiston was incorrect in assuming the brief partial eclipse in 4 BCE was the one referred to by Josephus.

It will become obvious why neither a *5 BCE nor a 6 BCE birth* can be reconciled with any of the traditional doctrines.

Chapter Nineteen

Breaking news: A new slant on an old tradition

This heading is occasioned by the recently retired Pope's admission that he believes the Roman Catholic Church's BC doctrine relating to the time of the Messiah's birth is incorrect.

The ex-Pope's disclosure that he believed **Yaishua** was born in an earlier year than the church has historically proclaimed for so long appears in his recently published book (late 2012), and since books don't materialize overnight, he must have subscribed to this belief for some time during his tenure as leader of the church.

This raises the questions:

Why had the Pope (and others in his confidence in the hierarchy of the church with whom he would have surely discussed these matters), not announced it to the church at large prior to its publication while he was acting as pontiff solely responsible for church doctrine?

Was this a contributing reason for his sudden retirement? Because not only did he no longer believe the traditional teaching of the organization on this issue, but he must have also recognized the impact this would have upon the church's doctrine of the death and resurrection, surely making his position as Pope untenable.

It is likely that his opinion is based upon the popular belief that Herod, who was responsible for killing the infants 2 years old and younger in an attempt to murder the Messiah, died in *4 BCE*.

The Pope was simply stating the obvious—that Herod couldn't have died before the year that the Church claimed the Messiah was born in.

This issue exposes the fragility of the 'first day of the week' resurrection hypothesis, because if the birth year is changed so also must the year and day of death be altered accordingly, therefore it is worth examining in a little more detail.

The traditional Roman Catholic doctrine, which is also embraced by a large majority of Sunday-keeping Protestant assemblies (remember that King James was a defender of this part of the faith), is based upon the following:

i) **Yaishua's** birth took place on 25 December *2 BCE*.

ii) He was 30 years old at the time of His baptism, which in that case would have taken place on or about 25 December AD 29.

iii) His ministry was approximately three and a quarter years long; therefore, it proposes that He would have died on Good Friday and would have been resurrected on Easter Sunday morning in *33 CE*, in His thirty-fourth year.

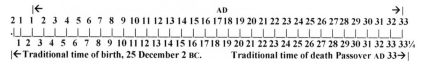

It should be clear that the Pope's 'new revelation' must refer to a year *earlier* than **5** BC. If it is believed Herod died before a Passover festival following an eclipse of the moon earlier in *4 BCE* and since the Roman Catholic Church claims that **Yaishua** was born on 25 December, if this were to have occurred in *5 BCE*, He would have been about *8 weeks old* at the time of Herod's death and the infants would have been massacred before that time while the infant **Yaishua** *was still in Bethlehem.*

Clearly, neither of these options are credible. Consequently, we will continue on the basis that the ex-Pope's conjecture is based upon a 6 BCE birth.

If the status quo were to prevail according to the church's traditional doctrine (i.e. **Yaishua's** baptism at 30 years of age, His three-and-a-quarter-year ministry, and His death in **33** CE), the answers to the following issues need to be addressed:

i) If **Yaishua** *was* born in 6 BCE instead of the traditional 2 BCE (a difference of four years), the year of His death and resurrection must be correspondingly altered (i.e. from Passover in 33 CE to Passover in 29 CE).

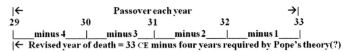

```
|←            Passover each year              →|
29              30              31              32              33
|___minus 4___|___minus 3___|___minus 2___|___minus 1___|
|← Revised year of death = 33 CE minus four years required by Pope's theory(?)
```

```
|← BCE →| |←                               CE                                →|
6 5 4 3 2 1 1 2 3 4 5 6 7 8 9 10 11 12 13 14 15 16 17 18 19 20 21 22 23 24 25 26 27 28 29
·L·|__|__|__|__|__|__|__|__|__|__|__|__|__|__|__|__|__|__|__|__|__|__|__|__|__|__|__|__|
  1 2 3 4 5 6 7 8 9 10 11 12 13 14 15 16 17 18 19 20 21 22 23 24 25 26 27 28 29 30 31 32 33 33¼
|←Revised time of birth, 25 December 6 BCE.        Revised time of death Passover 29 CE→↑
```

According to astronomical calculations, Passover in *29 CE* began on Saturday, 16 April, which according to Roman Catholic reckoning (three 'days' and two nights in the heart of the earth) would in turn mean the crucifixion took place in the afternoon of *Sunday* and the resurrection on *Tuesday morning*!

In Roman Catholic terminology, this in effect means that the ex-Pope now believes that **Yaishua** died on 'Good Sunday' and was resurrected on 'Easter Tuesday' morning!

ii) If **Yaishua** did die at the time of Passover in 29 CE, following an approximate three-and-a-quarter-year ministry, He would have been baptized on or about 25 December 25 CE, aged 'about thirty' (Luke 3:23) and John the Baptist would have been commissioned about six months earlier, neither of which have any remote connection to the fifteenth year of Tiberius's government:

```
25 December →|          |←            Passover each year              →|
         25        26              27              28              29
         |_____|_____|_____|_____|
   Baptism →|←               approx. 3¼ years                       →|
```

iii) If **Yaishua** *was* baptized in **25** CE, and died in **33** CE as is traditionally claimed, His ministry would have been about **seven and a quarter years long**.

```
25 December→|       |←                Passovers                     →|
  Baptism → 25    26      27      28      29      30      31      32      33
            | ¼  | 1¼ yrs | 2¼ yrs | 3¼ yrs | 4¼ yrs | 5¼ yrs | 6¼ yrs | 7¼ yrs |
                                                                    Death →|
```

iv) In that case, He would have died in His thirty-eighth year.

```
|←                              25 December                            →|
6 5 4 3 2 1 1 2 3 4  5  6   7   8  9  10 11 12 13 14 15 16 17 18  19 20 21 22 23 24 25 26 27 28 29 30 31 32 33
|LLLLLLLLL|_|_|_|_|_|_|_|_|_|_|_|_|_|_|_|_|_|_|_|_|_|_|_|_|_|_|_|_|_|_|_|
 1 2 3 4 5 6 7 8 9 10 11 12 13 14 15 16 17 18 19 20 21 22 23 24 25 26 27 28 29 30 31 32 33 34 35 36 37
|← Birth 25 December 6 BCE          in 38ᵗʰ year at death, Passover 33 CE →↑
```

v) On the other hand, if He was born in 6 BCE and was baptized in 29 CE according to tradition, He would have been about 34 years old at the time of baptism. This makes for a tenuous connection to Luke's 'about thirty'.

```
|←                        25 December                          →|
25      26      27      28      29      30      31      32      33
30      31      32      33      34 ← age at baptism      death →|
                        |← 'about thirty'(?)     Passover →|
```

vi) Since John the Baptist was commissioned at least six months before **Yaishua** was baptized, if this were in AD 25, John could not have been commissioned in the fifteenth year of the government of Tiberius Caesar as Luke says he was.

As a result, this would mean that Tiberius's first year would have begun in 11 CE:

```
|← Pope's revised 1st    and    15th years of Tiberius' government CE →|    |
11   12   13   14   15   16   17   18   19   20   21   22   23   24   25   26   27   28   29
| 1st | 2nd | 3rd | 4th | 5th | 6th | 7th | 8th | 9th | 10th | 11th | 12th | 13th | 14th | 15th | 16th | 17th | 18th |
        | 1st | 2nd | 3rd | 4th | 5th | 6th | 7th | 8th | 9th | 10th | 11th | 12th | 13th | 14th | 15th |
        |← Historical beginning    and    15th year of Tiberius' government →|    |
```

It is surprising that there has been little apparent concern about the ramifications of the ex-Pope's belief since it directly challenges the long-standing Roman Catholic theology regarding the death and resurrection of the Messiah.

Because it hasn't been, it highlights the fact that even after the magnitude of these claimed errors in the traditional doctrinal beliefs was acknowledged by the highest authority in the church, it is business as usual without even a ripple of concern.

Unsurprisingly, Protestant organizations that have adopted traditional Roman Catholic theology have also had little insightful input into this matter. From the deafening silence, it seems few, if any, of either group are very much concerned; perhaps they feel that it simply doesn't matter.

We shall discuss this matter in the next chapter.

Obviously, for every year earlier the birth is claimed to have taken place the problem is exacerbated. This applies to all alternative hypotheses, not only that of the Roman Catholic persuasion, and makes the problem of the confusing array of doctrinal beliefs currently before us even more difficult to comprehend.

Chapter Twenty

The Fourth Commandment or the 'Christian' Sabbath

This brings us to the following issue:

If **Yaishua** was not resurrected on Easter Sunday, why has the Sabbath, the fourth of the Ten Commandments, been replaced in general Christian worship by the first day of the week, Sunday?

Of the ten, nine are never questioned; the one that *is* constantly disputed is the fourth.

CVOT: 'You are to remember the sabbath day to hallow it. Six days shall you serve and do all your work, yet the seventh day is a sabbath to Yahweh your Elohim (God)' (Exodus 19:8).

Considering the evidence presented throughout 'The Trial', any argument based upon scriptural grounds (as opposed to biblical reasoning) for a Sunday resurrection and consequent Christian Sabbath is baseless.

The following points are quite clear:

By blessing the seventh-day and hallowing it, **YHWH** set it apart from all other days of the week:

CVOT: 'And finishing is the Elohim on the sixth day His work which He does. And ceasing is He on the seventh day from His work which He does. And blessing is the Elohim the seventh day and hallowing it, for in it He ceases from all His work, which the ELOHIM creates to make' (Genesis 2:1-3).

This is the same day of the week recorded in the Ten 'Words' (Commandments) written by the finger of **YHWH** on stone tablets as part of the covenant He made on Mount Horeb in Arabia (Galatians 4:25).

This is the same Sabbath day that **Yaishua** said He *is* Lord of and taught His followers and others how to observe.

CLNT: 'Now if you had known what this is: Mercy am I wanting and not sacrifice—you would not convict the faultless, for the Son of Man(kind) *is* Lord of the sabbath' (Matthew 12:7-8, refer also to Luke 6:5).

There is no question whatsoever that **Yaishua** was referring to the seventh-day Sabbath because the people He was addressing were all seventh-day Sabbath-observant Jews, both disciples and non-believers in **Yaishua** as the promised Messiah, who could only have understood Him to be referring to the seventh-day Sabbath.

He never intimated that He was Lord of any day other than the seventh-day Sabbath, and if, as the 'first day of the week' doctrine proclaims, the seventh-day Sabbath was annulled shortly after He made the above statement, it was/is meaningless.

To the contrary, He reinforced the above statement to these very first Christians that Sabbaths would still be in operation *after* His death and resurrection when He warned them:

CLNT: 'Now be praying that your flight may not be occurring in winter, nor yet on a sabbath' (Matthew 24:15-21).

Since **Yaishua** is Lord of the seventh-day Sabbath, He would not have instituted a different day, thereby contradicting His Father's words by establishing a Christian Sabbath as a memorial of His supposed resurrection on the fictitious 'first day of the week'.

Had He done so, since none of the Commandments can be annulled, this would have created a Sabbath weekend—Saturday and Sunday!

The Roman Catholic Church had not yet been established; consequently, neither had the 'first day of the week' resurrection, which it eventually created.

The scriptures reveal that both before and after the return of the Messiah, believers will be observing the seventh-day Sabbath.

Before:

CLNT: 'And the dragon is angry with the woman and came away to do battle with the rest of her seed, who are keeping the commandments of God and who have the testimony of Jesus' (Revelation 12:17, 14:12).

There can be no disagreement between the commandments of God and the testimony of **Yaishua**, whose testimony included the seventh-day Sabbath, a clear refutation of the illusory 'first day of the week' interpolation.

After:

CVOT: 'For just as the new heavens and the new earth which I shall make shall stand before Me, averring is **Yahweh**, so your seed and your name shall stand. And it will come to be, as often as the new moon comes in its monthly time and as often as the sabbath comes in its sabbath cycle, all flesh shall come to worship before Me, says **Yahweh**' (Isaiah 66:22-23).

At no time did **Yaishua** give any indication that the seventh-day Sabbath was to be deferred, annulled, or transferred. As our teacher, He would have been remiss if it was His intention to replace it but withheld that information from His followers, particularly in view of His own words:

CLNT: 'You should not infer that I came to demolish the law or the prophets. I came not to demolish but to fulfil. For verily I am saying to you: Till heaven and earth should be passing by, one iota or serif* may by no means be passing by from the law till all should be occurring. Whosoever, then, should be annulling one of the least of these precepts (commandments) and should be teaching men thus, the least in the kingdom of the heavens shall he be called' (Matthew 5:17-19).

* **NASB**: 'Smallest letter stroke', with footnote: Lit., *'one iota* (yohd) or *one projection of a letter* (serif)'. **RSV**: 'Not an iota, not a dot.'

Leaving aside the extent of the law referred to in the above text, it must be obvious that at least it included all the Ten Commandments.

As a result, those who have taught that the 'first day of the week' is the Sabbath Christians should observe have caused sincere Christians to reject the God-given Sabbath of the Fourth Commandment, the memorial of God's creation.

The prosecution has clearly shown that after almost 2,000 years of Sunday 'Christian Sabbath' observance, some other reason must now be provided to justify this observance.

Sunday-keeping Christians justify their belief on the basis that they are obeying the law God has inscribed on their hearts, including the unwritten 'first day of the week', the Sunday 'Sabbath'.

So where does that leave seventh-day-Sabbath keepers who believe they too are obeying the laws written by God on their hearts, including the scriptural Fourth Commandment?

You would surely agree that the laws God has inscribed upon their hearts **cannot** contradict or annul His written Word. One would have thought that all ten of the Commandments written on the hearts of all Christians would at least be the same.

Whilst seventh-day-Sabbath keepers base their belief on the command written in the scriptures, they are often pilloried for being legalistic by following a Jewish law.

Yaishua was repeatedly accused by religious Jews of breaking their man-made Sabbath legalisms by healing, helping, raising people from the dead, and even picking ears of grain to eat on the Sabbath!

In all the reported dealings **Yaishua** had on Sabbaths, none indicate He had a legalistic theology regarding its observance.

But are Sunday-keepers any less legalistic?

The Roman Catholic Church cannot claim to be because they have condemned people to 'hell' for not attending their Sunday ritual services and other church-imposed laws. It surely can't get much more legalistic than that!

Sunday-keepers who pontificate about others who observe the command written in their hearts to set apart the seventh-day scriptural Sabbath reveal the legalistic mind-set they accuse Sabbath-keepers of having.

To believe that the seventh-day Sabbath is an onerous command in the Jewish law by implication is to also believe that all the Ten Commandments are Jewish (and equally onerous); therefore, the other commandments must also only be applicable to Jews. Such a view is patently absurd.

This view of legalism historically attached to the Sabbath has its roots in anti-Semitism and to this day is, as it was then, frequently referred to as the 'Jewish' Sabbath.

This anti-Semitism is certainly evident in the words of Constantine (who has had such an enduring influence on Christian doctrines), who wrote regarding 'Easter':

> It was, in the first place, declared improper to follow the custom of the Jews in the celebration of this Holy festival*, because, their hands being stained with crime, the minds of these wretched men are necessarily blinded. Let us then have nothing in common with the Jews, who are our adversaries . . . who after having compassed the death of our Lord, being out of their minds, are guided not by sound reason but by an unrestrained passion, wherever their innate madness carries them . . . a people so utterly depraved . . . therefore this irregularity must be corrected in order that we no more have anything in common with those parricides and the murderers of our Lord.

* The Jewish Passover coinciding with Easter which, considering Constantine's unbalanced invectives, was obviously well entrenched in his time.

It is not surprising that subsequent church councils resolved that if the Paschal full moon should occur on a Sunday and thereby coincide with the Passover festival, Easter should be commemorated on the following Sunday.

Neither is it any wonder that Constantine earlier gave formal recognition to Sunday by his edict of 7 March 321 CE:

> Let all judges and townspeople and the occupation of all trades rest on the venerable day of the sun.

He did not have in mind the Son!

As a result of these attempts to distance Christianity from what was perceived as Judaism, many Christians now include in their celebrations the pagan customs associated with the festival of Easter, named after a pagan fertility goddess (as evidenced by the fertility symbols of Easter eggs and Easter bunnies at the time of **Yaishua's** purported resurrection).

This is in spite of **YHWH's** instruction:

CVOT: 'Thus says **Yahweh**: "The way of the nations do not learn"' (Jeremiah 10:2).

The lackadaisical, preconceived doctrinal approach to scriptural translation, which has been clearly identified throughout 'The Trial', is further evident in the **KJV**:

> And when he had apprehended him, he put him in prison . . . intending after Easter to bring him forth to the people. (Acts 12:4)

The scriptural text that this interpretation supposedly represents contains the obviously correct Passover, not Easter. As a result of this mischievous misinterpretation, those believers who currently include Easter as a Christian festival can now claim biblical authority in defence of its observance! **KJV** biblical authority it may be, but it certainly isn't scriptural truth!

This error has directly resulted in the inclusion of customs associated with and named after a pagan goddess of fertility, variously named as Astarte, Eostre, etc., depending upon the culture that has adopted it.

Traditional Christian organisations (churches) have long compromised scriptural truth by their associations with paganism, like 'Christmas' and 'Easter'. Surely the time has come (and has always been) when truth-seeking Christians spurn these associations, no matter how unpopular or unpalatable that might be with 'churchianity' and those who prefer to follow its dictates (remember the Bereans) and stand up for scriptural truth as the apostle Paul entreated.

> **CLNT:** 'For the rest brethren, whatever is true, whatever is grave, whatever is just, whatever is pure, whatever is agreeable, whatever is renowned—if there is any virtue, and if any applause, be taking these into account . . .' (Philippians 4:8).

> **CLNT:** Endeavour to present yourself to God qualified, an unashamed worker, correctly cutting the word of truth . . .' (2 Timothy 2:15).

Having read through 'The Trial', it should be evident to you that today God's grace is experienced by Sabbath-keepers and Sunday-keepers alike because had the penalties required by the law of Moses been applied, many/most would have been executed by now! It is a misconception to believe that by honouring God's laws, one is not able to receive His grace or to be gracious to others.

Christians and Jews (should) stand distinct from other-god believers because they have knowledge of the only true God's* will for mankind, enabling them to conduct themselves accordingly.

*John 17:3

The Ten Commandments form a fundamental basis of godly behaviour, which surely should be common to both Jews and Christians alike since we believe in the same God.

Although you have seen that there is no scriptural evidence to support the replacement of the seventh-day Sabbath, the Roman Catholic Church openly boasts that it has the authority for establishing it's replacement.

For example:

> 'Q: How prove you that the Church has power to command feasts and holidays?
> A: By the very act of changing the Sabbath into Sunday, which Protestants allow of . . .
>
> Q: How prove you this?
> A: Because by keeping Sunday they acknowledge the Church's power to ordain feasts.' (An Abridgement of Christian Doctrine)

'The word of God commandeth the seventh day to be the
Sabbath of the Lord, and to be kept holy; you (Protestants),
without any precept of scripture, change it to the first day
of the week, only authorized by our traditions.' (Treatise of
Thirty Controversies)

Protestants have frequently acknowledged their obedience to these
traditional edicts enacted by the Roman Catholic Church:

'The seventh day, the commandment says, is the Sabbath
of the Lord thy God. No kind of arithmetic, no kind of
almanac can make seven equal to one, or the seventh mean
the first, nor Saturday mean Sunday . . . The fact is that
we are all Sabbath-breakers, every one of us.' (Rev. George
Hodges, Episcopal Dispatch)

The above abbreviated excerpts are from The resurrection—When?
by Ithamar Quigley (published by The Bible Sabbath Association,
Fairview, Oklahoma).

These honest appraisals agree that the belief in a Sunday resurrection
provides no reason whatsoever for replacing the Sabbath of the Ten
Commandments. They support the view that there is no scriptural
command to annul the Sabbath nor to keep it holy (set apart) because
it was never changed from the seventh-day Sabbath to the mythical
man-made substitute 'first day of the week' Christian Sabbath in the
mistaken belief that **Yaishua** was resurrected on that day.

Simple logic should tell us that if none of the other Ten Commandments written by the finger of God have changed, why should it be believed that the fourth has?

Paul's entreaty to Timothy should apply to us all.

CLNT: 'Endeavour to present yourself to God qualified, an unashamed worker, correctly cutting the word of truth' (2 Timothy 2:15).

Yaishua's actions and teaching on how the Sabbath may be observed are clearly revealed in the New Testament.

CLNT: 'The sabbath came because of mankind and not mankind because of the sabbath, so that the Son of Man*kind* is Lord also of the sabbath' (Mark 2:27).

CLNT: 'And He entered again into the synagogue and a man was there, having a withered hand. And they scrutinized Him to see if on the sabbaths He will be curing him, that they should be accusing Him. And He is saying to the man having the withered hand: "Rise in the midst". And He is saying to them: "Is it allowed on the sabbaths to do good or to do evil, a soul to save or kill?". Yet they were silent . . . And coming out, the Pharisees hold a consultation with the Herodians against Him, so that they should be destroying Him' (Mark 3:1-6).

CLNT: 'At that season Jesus went through the sowings on the sabbaths. Now His disciples hunger and they begin to be plucking the ears and to be eating. Now the Pharisees, perceiving it, say to Him: Lo! Your disciples are doing what is not allowed to be done on a sabbath' (Matthew 12:1-2).

CLNT: 'Let no one, then, be judging you in food or drink or the particulars of a festival, or of new moons, or of sabbaths, which are* a shadow of those things which are impending' (Colossians 2:16: Paul).

* Not 'were'.

Personally, when reading these accounts and others, freedom comes to mind—freedom from traditional man-made customs, rituals, and strictures, not legalisms.

Therein lies the wonderful grace of our God and His Son; you are not answerable in the judgement to church doctrines but to **YHWH** and **Yaishua**.

CLNT: 'For other foundation can no one lay beside that which is laid, which is Jesus Christ. Now if anyone is building on this foundation gold and silver, precious stone, wood, grass, straw, each one's work will become apparent, for the day will make it evident, for it is being revealed by fire and the fire, it will be testing each one's work—what kind it is. If anyone's work will be remaining which he builds on it, he will get wages. If anyone's work shall be burned up he will forfeit it, yet he shall be saved, yet thus: as through fire' (1 Corinthians 3:11-15).

Conclusion

It is taken for granted that our bibles are accurate accounts of the events recorded in the ancient (source) documents, and for the most part, they are.

However, in addressing the subject of the death and resurrection in 'The Trial', it has been revealed that this is not always the case.

J. F. Bethuane-Baker comments: 'As soon as ever men went beyond the simple phrases of the apostolic writers and, instead of merely repeating by rote the scriptural words and terms, tried to express in their own language the great facts of their faith, they naturally often used terms which were inadequate—which, if not positively misleading, erred by omission and defect.'

(An Introduction to the Early History of Christian Doctrine by J. F. Bethuane-Baker, DD. Fifth Edition Revised. Published by Methuan & Co. LTD, 36 Essex Street WC, London.)

It has been clearly shown that when compared with a literal translation of the ancient Greek manuscripts regarding the death and resurrection of the Son of God, key texts have been modified or omitted, to fit the popular 'first day of the week' doctrine, with the result that most Christians now believe these alterations are literal accounts of the original texts.

The literal facts are both clearly written and simple to understand and require no modification, either by altering the meaning of words or removing them or adding words to conform the texts to the traditional doctrines. This bears out the common sense apparent in the oft-repeated comment 'If the literal sense makes sense, seek no other sense'.

The process began very early in church history, and it is now taken for granted with little or no current opposition that these doctrines must be true, in spite of the fact that these corrections continue to play a significant part in the historical development of schisms throughout Christendom as they have always done.

When one considers the penalties that the Roman Catholic Church purported to have the authority to inflict upon those who demurred against its doctrines throughout the ages (excommunication, loss of salvation, hellfire, shame, rigorous penances, exile, estrangement from family, etc.), it is little wonder that there was eventually little or no opposition to these traditional beliefs, particularly when they were claimed to be supported by the Holy Bible.

Fortunately, the scribes involved in copying from the source manuscripts, who produced the three ancient texts used in 'The Trial', all faithfully retained the integrity of those source texts. Considering that these were copies (probably of copies), it is significant that all three codices retained the obviously original 'one of the sabbaths'.

Unfortunately, that scribal integrity was destroyed when theologians took it upon themselves to interpret 'sabbaton' (Sabbath) to 'week' to conform to an already believed doctrine. This has always been the strong point in the transmission of the Hebrew texts throughout the ages, which—although they could never be perfect replicas of the ancient source texts—had processes in place that prevented significant variations from developing over long periods of time.

Refusing to acknowledge these errors on the weak argument of longevity is one thing, but to do so against the weight of evidence submitted throughout 'The Trial' is nothing other than an endorsement of the authority of the founders of this process.

We now know that the recently retired Pope ironically no longer supports the church's historical doctrine of the year of the birth of the Son of God, which also highlights the error of its doctrine on the days of His death and resurrection.

'The Trial' has simply exposed the tip of the iceberg, for there are many other traditional doctrinal beliefs that fail to match up to the scriptural fine print.

In spite of this, the systematic doctrinal bias of the common interpretations that appear in many bibles today, which is so evident throughout 'The Trial', has purged the scriptures of any post-resurrection connection with the so-called Jewish Sabbath. In so doing, Christianity has been separated from its inescapable Jewish roots.

As a result of the misinterpretations identified throughout 'The Trial', in effect there are now two sets of Ten Commandments—the Jewish set containing the seventh-day Sabbath and the Gentile set containing 'the first day of the week'.

Since the meaning of 'holy' is (to be) 'separate' or 'set apart', how can unbelievers be expected to understand and follow scriptural truth when many supposed believers publicly demonstrate their affinity with pagan traditions founded on the false premise that their Saviour was raised from the dead on Easter Sunday?

In that context, how much more meaningful are **Yaishua**'s words in Matthew 5:13:

CLNT: 'You are the salt of the earth. Now if the salt should be made insipid, with what will it be salted.'

Here are a few other scriptures you may wish to reflect on:

CLNT: 'For not by following wisely made myths do we make known to you the power and presence of our Lord Jesus Christ' (2 Peter 1:16).

CLNT: 'In this is love perfected with us, that we may have boldness in the day of judging, seeing that according as He is so are we in this world' (1 John 4:17).

CLNT: 'I am not asking that You should be taking them out of the world, but that You should be keeping them from the wicked one. Of the world they are not, according as I am not of the world. Hallow them by your truth. Your word is truth' (John 17:15).

CLNT: 'I am conjuring you in the sight of God and Christ Jesus Who is about to be judging the living and the dead, in accord with His advent and His kingdom: Herald the word. Stand by it, opportunely, inopportunely, expose, rebuke, entreat, with all patience and teaching. For the era will be when they will not tolerate sound teaching, but, their hearing being tickled, they will heap up for themselves teachers in accord with their own desires and indeed they will be turning their hearing away from the truth, yet will be turned aside to myths' (2 Timothy 4:1-4).

Many today recognize and distance themselves from anti-Semitism, yet those who promote the glaringly disingenuous 'first day of the week' are unwittingly promoting a doctrine that has its roots in anti-Semitic replacement theology by distancing Christianity from the so-called Jewish Sabbath.

All true Christians believe that **Yaishua** died and was resurrected from the dead (Romans 10:6-10), so does it really matter on which days He died and was resurrected?

Because of the divisions that have developed between Christians, one of which (the subject of 'The Trial') has resulted in the annulment of the Sabbath, the answer has to be a resounding **'Yes'**.

A word of gratitude must be offered here to the Concordant Literal Version of the scriptures, which has endeavoured to uphold the consistent literal integrity of the source texts on which it is founded.

Sadly, sincere Christians today believe they are obeying the Creator's command to 'remember the sabbath day, to hallow it' by observing the replacement man-made, un-scriptural first day of the week, the Christian Sabbath, in honour of the Saviour because that is the day they have been misled to believe He was resurrected on.

The prosecution asserts that it is critically important; if the evidence submitted throughout 'The Trial' has resulted in a 'guilty as charged' verdict, you have an obligation to act accordingly.

Epilogue

Considering that the Gospels are derived from 1st, 2nd and 3rd-hand accounts, it should not be surprising that there appears to be some discrepancies between them.

Arguably, one of the most obvious of the apparent disagreements between the Gospels is the differing descriptions of the visit (or visits) to the tomb. For instance:

	Matthew	Mark	Luke	John
Time:	evening before one of the Sabbaths	sunrise on one of the Sabbaths	in the early depths of one of the Sabbaths	morning, still dark, on one of the Sabbaths
Who:	Mary Magdalene +Mary	the women +Salome	the women +others	Mary Magdalene
Spices:	not mentioned	bought spices*	prepare spices*	women witnessed spices applied before burial
The stone:	in place	rolled away	rolled away	rolled away

Next:	saw **Yaishua** Who spoke to them held Yaishua's feet	fled from tomb, spoke to no one He appeared to Mary Magdalene	reported to the eleven He wasn't seen	told Peter and John. Mary Magdalene returned to the tomb saw Him. He said 'Don't touch Me'
Messengers:	one	one	two	two
Where:	outside tomb	inside tomb	inside tomb	inside tomb
Status:	risen	risen	risen	risen

* Preparing spices took a considerable length of time, making it impossible to have observed **Yaishua**'s burial on Good Friday (or Saturday as amended by astronomical calculations), purchased the spices, prepared them, rested on the Sabbath, and been at the tomb at approximately 6 a.m. on Easter Sunday morning.

Matthew identified the reason the women visited the tomb shortly before sunset was 'to behold the tomb', with no mention of spices.

Because John had previously given a detailed explanation that **Yaishua's** body was prepared for burial with the myrrh and aloes, 'according as the custom of the Jews is to bury', he understandably omitted any mention of spices when the tomb was later visited.

He also omitted any mention of the women being present at the time the body was prepared for burial by Joseph and Nicodemus but supports Mark's statement in 16:9 that in the morning of 'one of the sabbaths', Mary Magdalene was alone when she visited the tomb, yet Mark earlier stated that the women and Salome were present.

John indicates that at that time the stone was already rolled away from the entrance to the tomb, as Mark and Luke do, whereas Matthew reveals that the women were present when a heavenly messenger rolled the stone from its entrance.

Matthew and Mark both state that Mary Magdalene was present when the body was placed in the tomb and the stone rolled over the entrance.

Mark says that Mary Magdalene and Mary, the mother of James and Salome, brought spices 'that they should be rubbing Him', which Mark states occurred after the (festival) Sabbath. Luke states that 'the women who were come together out of Galilee with Him, gaze at the tomb and how His body was placed and after returning they made ready spices and attars and on the (festival) sabbath indeed they are quiet according to the precept'.

These resurrection accounts obviously contain some inconsistencies and beg the question, why would the women prepare spices to rub the body whilst having to face the danger of attempting the seemingly impossible task of removing the guarded and sealed stone which Mark describes as being 'tremendously great' ('sphodra mega', **KJV:** 'very great'), when they had observed that Joseph and Nicodemus had already bound **Yaishua's** body 'in swathings with the spices, according as the custom of the Jews is to bury'?

There are several speculative theories about these differences; however, there is one overriding consideration—in every account, the visitors were told that **Yaishua** was already resurrected.

There are sound scriptural reasons why Matthew's was the earliest of the accounts in chronological order of the events.

i)   The stone was still in place when the women came to the tomb, whereas the other accounts record that it was already rolled away.

ii) Because **Yaishua** died at the ninth hour (3 p.m.), was buried immediately before sunset, and was 'in the heart of the earth for three days and three nights' as He said, it would require the resurrection to have taken place before sunset after three days and three nights had elapsed. Had He been resurrected the following morning, He would have been dead for three and a half days and four nights.

iii) **CLNT:** 'Now rising, in the morning in the first sabbath He appeared first to Mary Magdalene' (Mark 16:9). 'Rising' is written in the aorist tense, indicating that the event had already taken place without identifying the exact time, which has been revealed as being close to the previous sunset at the time of 'lighting up' into 'one of the sabbaths' (Matthew 28:1).

iv) Because Mark 16:9 clearly reveals that **Yaishua** appeared to Mary Magdalene in the morning of the first (seventh-day) Sabbath, the resurrection must have taken place before both Sunday morning and Saturday afternoon.

Consequently, there is merit in the suggestion that the accounts are describing different visits to the tomb.

CNLT: 'But surely, together with all these things also, it is leading in this third day since these things occurred' (Luke 23:21).

Instead of '*it is leading in this third day since these things occurred*', the sublinear of the **Concordant Interlinear Greek scriptures** contains the following literal translation:

> *But surely and together to-all these third this day it-is-leading*
> *from* which these became.*

*Strong's no. 575 states: '"Apo": a primary particle; "off", i.e. away (from something near), in various senses (of place, time, or relation; lit. or fig.):- (x here-) after, ago, at, because of, before, by the space of, for (-th), from, in, (out) of, off, (up-) on (-ce), since, with. In composition (as a prefix) it usually denotes separation departure, cessation, completion, reversal, etc.'

Remember that this conversation took place in the late afternoon of 'one of the sabbaths'. Consequently, it cannot be construed to support either a Sabbath afternoon or Sunday morning resurrection.

Because of this and the reasons previously given, it is taken to read:

> But surely, together with all these things also it is leading
> from this third day in which these things occurred.

Teachers of the traditional 'first day of the week' doctrine claim other texts support the belief that the Sabbath has been replaced. For instance:

CLNT: 'Now the infirm in the faith be taking to yourselves, but not for discrimination of reasonings. One indeed is believing to eat all things, yet the infirm one is eating greens. Let not him who is eating be scorning him who is not eating. Yet let not him who is not eating be judging him who is eating, for God took him to Himself. Who are you to be judging another's domestic? To his own Master he is standing or falling.

'One indeed is deciding* for one day rather than another day, yet one is deciding for every day.

'Let each one be fully assured in his own mind. He who is disposed to the day, is disposed to it to the Lord; and he who is eating, is eating to the Lord, for he is thanking God. And he who is not eating, to the Lord is not eating and is thanking God and he who is not eating, to the Lord is not eating and is thanking God . . .

'Now why are you judging your brother? Or why are you scorning your brother? For all of us shall be presented at the dais of God . . . Consequently then, each of us shall be giving an account concerning himself to God.

'By no means, then, should we still be judging one another, but rather decide this: not to place a stumbling block for a brother or a snare.

I have perceived and am persuaded in the Lord Jesus that nothing is contaminating of itself, except that the one reckoning anything to be contaminating, to that one it is contaminating.

'For if because of food, your brother is sorrowing, you are no longer walking according to love. Do not, by your food, destroy that one for whose sake Christ died. Let not then your good be calumniated for the kingdom of God is not food and drink, but righteousness and peace and joy in holy spirit.

'For he who in this is slaving for Christ is well pleasing to God and attested by men. Consequently then we are pursuing peace and the edification of one another.

'Not on account of food demolish the work of God. All indeed is clean, but it is evil to the man who with stumbling is eating. It is ideal not to be eating meat, nor yet to be drinking wine, nor yet to do aught by which your brother is stumbling, or is being snared or weakened.

'The faith which you have, have for yourself in God's sight . . . Now he who is doubting if he should be eating is condemned, seeing that it is not out of faith. Now everything which is not out of faith is sin' (Romans 14).

This entire passage is referring to food, what or when one eats or abstains from eating, and that it is not up to others to judge. It has absolutely no connection to a replacement of the Sabbath; in fact, had it been recognised that nowhere do the scriptures record a *first day of the week* resurrection, this text would not be cited to support the belief that it did!

* The Greek word used in this passage, 'krino' ('to make a decision, come to a conclusion'), is translated by the **KJV** as 'esteemeth', giving the impression that it may have some connection to a day that was esteemed, e.g. a Sabbath. However, it is folly to believe that one could be esteeming every day as a Sabbath. Paul, who himself worked for a living, knew fellow believers had to do so also.

The same comment applies to Colossians 2:16-23.

CLNT: 'Let no one then be judging you in food or in drink or in the particulars of a festival, or of a new moon, or of Sabbaths, which are a shadow of those things which are impending—yet the body is the Christ's . . . If then you died together with the Christ from the elements of the world, why as living in the world are you subject to decrees: "You should not be touching, nor yet tasting, nor yet coming into contact" (which things are all from corruption from use), in accord with the directions and teachings of men?' (Ref. Matthew 15:8-9).

Consistent with Romans 14, Paul is stressing that how, when, and why one chooses to observe these elements is between them and God only. Note that he uses the present tense '*are* a shadow', not '*were* a shadow'.

To claim that this text refers to the annulment of the Sabbath makes no sense because in a text that is generally considered to be referring to the millennial reign of the Messiah, it is evident that not only will the seventh-day Sabbath be in operation but so also will the Jewish calendar.

CVOT: 'For just as the new heavens and the new earth, which I shall make, shall stand before Me, averring is **Yahweh**, so your seed and your name shall stand. And it will come to be, as often as the new moon comes in its monthly time and as often as the sabbath in its sabbath cycle, all flesh shall come to worship before Me, says **Yahweh**' (Isaiah 66:22-23).

YHWH was addressing Israel through the prophet Isaiah, so there is no prize for guessing what Sabbaths are referred to in this text.

In addition, Zechariah 14:16 refers to the same time as Isaiah:

CVOT: 'And it will come to be that everyone left of the nations coming against Jerusalem will also go up, as often as year by year, to worship the King, **Yahweh** of hosts, and to celebrate the Festival of Booths.'

To suggest that Paul was aiding and abetting the annulment of the Sabbath or festivals in Colossians is reading a meaning into the text (eisegesis) to either claim the annulment of the Sabbath, the law, and/or the festivals. If they have this view, they should not use this text to support it.

When Paul attended synagogues, it was invariably on the Sabbaths. Had he argued that the Sabbath had been changed to 'the first day of the week', he would undoubtedly have very soon been harmed or killed.

This is not indicated anywhere in the scriptures and infers that Paul was a hypocrite by attending synagogue on Sabbath and then observing Sunday with Gentile Christians.

The word 'shadow' has nothing to do with annulment.

CLNT: 'For every chief priest is constituted to offer both approach presents and sacrifices. Whence it is necessary for This One also to have something to offer. Indeed then, if He were on earth He would not even be a priest, there being those who offer approach presents according to the law who, by an example and shadow, are offering the divine service of the celestials, according as Moses has been apprized when about to be completing the tabernacle. For, see, He is averring: that you shall be making all in accord with the model shown you in the mountain' (Hebrews 8:3-5).

The reference to 'shadow' is indicating that earthly models of pattern or service are representative (shadows or types) of those in the celestial kingdom, which is further explained in Hebrews 10:1:

CLNT: 'For the law, having a shadow of the impending good things, not the selfsame image of the matters, they with their same sacrifices which they are offering year by year, are never able to perfect to a finality those approaching.'

Those who believe that **Yaishua** annulled the Sabbath by supposedly being resurrected on Sunday have distorted the meaning of these texts to support their doctrine. Had believers clearly understood that the Sabbath had not been annulled or replaced with 'the first day of the week', they would never have come to the conclusion that the passages in Romans 14 and Colossians 2 were referring to the annulment or transference of the Sabbath, in effect negating the Commandment.

As was alluded to at the outset, the tentacles of tradition dictate the way such texts are currently understood.

CLNT: 'Are you not aware that a little leaven is leavening the whole kneading? Clean out then the old leaven that you may be a fresh kneading, according as you are unleavened. For our Passover also, Christ, was sacrificed for our sakes so that we may be keeping the festival, not with old leaven, nor yet with the leaven of evil and wickedness, but with unleavened sincerity and truth' (1 Corinthians 5:6-8).

Paul tells us that because **Yaishua** was/is our deliverer through being our Passover offering, *we may be keeping Passover* free of old leaven. 'Old leaven' is not the negation of the Passover festival with the introduction of the new Easter replacement theology, accompanied by the pomp and ceremony that many churches engage in at the time of the Easter festival (and other church-made festivals), which draws believers to participate.

It is hard to imagine how these grand rituals could ever be considered to be a reflection of **Yaishua**'s life and teaching.

Yaishua did not come to establish a divided religion but rather to teach us how to live our lives in a manner well pleasing to His Father, the only true GOD. As Peter explained:

CLNT: 'For this you were called, seeing that Christ also suffered for your sakes, leaving you a copy, that you should be following up in the footprints of Him Who does no sin, neither was guile found in His mouth; Who being reviled, reviled not again; suffering threatened not, yet gave it over to Him Who is judging justly, Who Himself carries up our sins in His body on to the pole, that coming away from sins we should be living for righteousness; by Whose welt you are healed' (1 Peter 2:21-24).

From the very beginning, the scriptures looked ahead to the appearance, death, and resurrection of God's own Son. For example:

CVOT: 'And creating is Elohim humanity in His image . . . And coming is it to be evening and coming to be morning, the sixth day' (Genesis 1:27, 31).

CLNT: 'Thus is it written also: The first man, Adam, became a living soul; the last Adam a vivifying Spirit' (1 Corinthians 15:45).

How incredible that the creation of Adam on the sixth day was foreshadowing the resurrection, the bringing back to life of 'the last Adam', **Yaishua**, on the sixth day thousands of years later!

However, that which has been in error from much earlier times remains in error for eternity; these errors can never be corrected simply by the passing of time.

Ultimately, we must give a personal account to the Just Judge according to the truth on our own behalf, not according to church doctrines. Obedience to incorrect doctrines will not be a defence on that day no matter how long they have been in existence, how popular they are, or how sincerely they are believed.

Some Personal Comments on Current Affairs

Many Christians today believe we are living in 'the last days', as described in many parts of both the Old and New Testaments. Those who were born a few decades ago have witnessed radical changes to the way we live, and if anything, the rate of change continues to accelerate.

Christians and non-Christians alike, are aware that many of these changes have had deleterious effects on societal values that were the norm but a few short years ago.

This view has been reinforced by relatively recent developments, which reveal that some scriptures that have historically been understood allegorically, now have the potential to be literal. For example:

CLNT: 'And whenever they should be finishing their testimony, the wild beast which is ascending out of the submerged chaos will be doing battle with them and will be conquering and killing them. And their corpses will be at the square of the great city, which, spiritually, is being called Sodom and Egypt, where their Lord, also, was crucified.

And those out of the peoples and tribes and languages and nations are observing their corpses three days and a half' (Revelation 11:7-13).

How else could this text have been understood other than allegorically? Yet since the advent of satellite television, people from around the globe are able to witness events taking place elsewhere on earth at the time that they take place, as the above text describes.

Similarly:

CLNT: 'And He [**Yaishua**, v. 30] shall be dispatching His messengers with a loud sounding trumpet, and they shall be assembling His chosen from the four winds, from the extremity of the heavens to their extremities' (Matthew 24:31).

Up until the latter part of the last century, there was no possibility for it to be believed that humans could be in *the extremity of the heavens*. However, in the last few decades, men have walked on the moon, the space station is continually inhabited, 'space tourists' will soon be a common occurrence, planning is taking place to conduct mining activities on the moon, and there is even a proposal for a permanent settlement on Mars (in spite of the fact that it is a one-way trip, there are over 1,000 people on the short list). It is now true that humans already exist in the *extremity of the heavens*, and there is the potential for those numbers to soon increase.

It has been reported that in 2013 about thirty-six million flights carried about *3.8 billion* people, it would be fair to say, throughout the 'extremities of the heavens' to their respective destinations (The New Zealand Herald, 10.03.2014). What was allegorically understood but a few decades ago are now everyday occurrences.

There are many other texts that also accurately identify events currently taking place. One of the responses **Yaishua** gave to the question 'What is the sign of Your presence and the conclusion of the eon?' was 'And because of the multiplication of lawlessness, the love of many shall be cooling' (Matthew 24:3, 12).

Who today would deny that because of increasing lawlessness 'the love of many is cooling'?

Governments throughout the world struggle with this problem. In many countries, one of the growth industries is the building of prisons to cater for the unprecedented numbers committed to serve their sentences in penal institutions. To help combat this situation, prison sentences are reduced, or alternative forms of confinement are imposed, such as home detention, because neither the prisons nor the courts can cope with the numbers before them.

Many governments in recent times have passed legislation legalising activities that just a few decades ago were not only considered to be illegal but also in some cases immoral, which today is destroying the moral fabric of societies.

Those legal and moral tenets of yesteryears have since been supplanted by those who today believe themselves to be more enlightened than those of earlier generations, who are either unaware of or wilfully ignore clear scriptural warnings not to follow such a path.

CVOT: 'Woe to those who are calling evil: 'good', and good: 'evil', placing darkness for light and light for darkness; placing bitter for sweet and sweet for bitter. Woe to those wise in their own eyes, and understanding in front of their own faces' (Isaiah 5:20-21).

KJV: 'Woe to those who are wise in their own eyes and prudent in their own sight!' (Isaiah 5:20-21).

The scriptures also warn:

CVOT: 'There is a way that seems upright before man, yet its end becomes the way of death' (Proverbs 14:12).

One example of the veracity of both of these texts is apparent in cases of abortion. The Commandment is quite clear: 'You shall not ***murder***.'

Murder is 'the act of putting a person to death intentionally and unlawfully*; excessive or reprehensible slaughter that is not legally murder' (Chambers Concise Dictionary).

It is often claimed that more infants have lost their lives whilst in their mothers' wombs since abortion was legalised than all deaths from all wars in that same period; one source claims as many as ***800 million*** abortions have been carried out since 1973*. That is quite believable considering that one doctor in the United States claims to have been responsible for about 1 million abortions.

*Totalitaria, by Ian Wishart. Published by Howling At The Moon Publishing Ltd, PO Box 188, Kaukapakapa, Auckland 0843, New Zealand.

*This explanation does not take into account that governments have *legalised* abortion; however, from a Christian standpoint, no government can 'legalise' what GOD has forbidden.

The 'wisdom' behind legalizing abortion stems from the misconception that the expected infant in its mother's womb is not considered to be a viable human being in the early stages of pregnancy; in some countries this even extends to late pregnancy.

It was recently reported in a local newspaper that in Spain in 2011 there were 118,000 terminations, an increase of 4.7 per cent from the previous year. The article reveals that the Spanish government wishes to limit the reasons for abortion procedures and thus drastically reduce that number (New Zealand Herald, 27.01.2014).

It is clear from the subheading and the article following that the negative response to this proposition is extremely emotive. The subheading reads: 'Proposal brings widespread condemnation at home and abroad and fears of rise in back-street terminations.' This of course totally and deliberately overlooks the fact that either way a baby's death is not an issue to be recognized.

The article later quotes one objector: 'Spain is facing tough times and using abortion, which causes so much suffering for women . . .'

That comment cannot be referring to the clinical procedures undertaken with the latest surgical techniques and equipment, which causes 'so much suffering for women', but rather to the fact that reliable scientific research indicates that in excess of 10 per cent of women who have had abortions suffer severe mental health issues later and that a far greater number overall also suffer long-term emotional/mental health disturbances.

In spite of the risk of this long-lasting suffering, some women have multiple abortions.

One would have thought that this well-intentioned proposal to at least reduce the number of abortions would receive support, not widespread condemnation, in view of the almost certain death of the infant (not all abortions are successful) and the high possibility of long-term mental health issues for the women.

Spain's existing law gives women the right to abort after fourteen weeks of pregnancy and twenty-two weeks if the woman's health is in danger or the foetus is seriously deformed.

That the Spanish government (believes it) can reduce the number of abortions reveals that the current law is being wrongly applied as a belated form of birth control, which gives the lie to the current legality of many of the 118,000 abortions.

It seems that the Spanish Government recognizes that many abortions do not meet the criteria required by current law. If that is the case, how many of them were endorsed by qualified medical practitioners sworn to uphold the law and protect human life?

The apostle Paul warned that 'in the last days, perilous periods will be present'. He described that one of the prevailing problems at that time would be that humans would be without natural affection (2 Timothy 3:1–3).

Few things surely could be more callous* than the wilful destruction of developing infants whilst in their mothers' wombs because a woman demanded the right to do whatever she wishes with her own body.

* Webster's Concise Dictionary: 'Hardened, unfeeling, cruel.'

A further article appeared in the New Zealand Herald (25.03.2014) with the headline:

'Hospital fetus scandal. Thousands of miscarried and aborted babies used to stoke hospital furnaces.'

The article went on to say: 'The bodies of thousands of aborted and miscarried babies were incinerated as clinical waste, with some used to heat Britain's hospitals, an investigation has found.'

As well as describing the bodies as *babies*, elsewhere in the article they were variously referred to as *clinical waste, rubbish, fetal remains, children and fetuses*. Do we dare call ourselves 'civilised' while we carry out such practices?

Women who become pregnant and look with expectation to the birth of their babies are often identified as 'mothers-to-be'. It is interesting to note that women who had a pregnancy terminated by voluntary abortion were described in the above article as 'mothers'; this is recognition that it was a living *baby* that had its life terminated.

There is surely a vast difference between a woman who wanted to give birth to the baby she was carrying but who tragically was unable to do so and her concern about what happened to its body and a woman who of her own volition decided to abort the child during its gestation period, simply because she demanded the right to do as she wished with her body, as the earlier article disclosed.

Many Christians who support abortion measures on compassionate grounds disagree with their church's stand on this* and other issues, which, measured by the reducing numbers of church members, reveals that many are now falling away from their faith, including the clergy, at a time when they are most needed.

* An article titled 'Polls show dislike for [Catholic] church rules' states in part: 'And 65 per cent said abortions should be allowed—8 percent in all cases, and 57 per cent in some cases' (New Zealand Herald, 11.02.2014, brackets added).

This apostasy has been foretold:

CLNT: 'Now we are asking you, brethren, for the sake of the presence of our Lord Jesus Christ and our assembling to Him, that you be not quickly shaken from your mind, nor yet be alarmed, either through spirit, or through word, or through an epistle as through us, as that the day of the Lord is present. No one should be deluding you by any method, for, should not the apostasy* be coming first?' (2 Thessalonians 2:1–5).

Apostasy: 'abandonment of one's religion, principles, or party; a revolt from ecclesiastical obedience, from a religious profession, or from holy orders; defection' (Chambers Concise Dictionary).

Those Christians (and non-Christians) who today refuse to compromise their scripturally based values are well aware that the battle between good and evil and/or right and wrong is raging.

They are also cognizant of the fact that a few short years ago the majority of people lived by the same values; however mankind has changed the 'rules', not God.

About 2,600 years ago, Daniel wrote:

CVOT: 'Now you Daniel, stop up the words and seal the scroll till the era of the end, when many will swerve as evil* will increase . . . for stopped up and sealed are the words till the era of the end. Many will purify and whiten themselves and be refined; yet the wicked will be wicked. None of all the wicked shall understand; yet the intelligent are understanding' (Daniel 12:4, 9).

KJV: 'But thou O Daniel, shut up the words and seal the book, even to the time of the end: many shall run to and fro, and knowledge* shall increase' (Daniel 12:4, 9).

* Hebrew 'da'ath': 'knowledge' (Langenscheidt Hebrew-English Dictionary, Strong's no. 1847).

The Concordant Literal Version indicates that 'evil' is conjecture but confirmed by the Septuagint. Either way, 'the intelligent' will understand that we have witnessed a phenomenal increase in both *evil* and *knowledge* in this generation.

Interestingly, **Yaishua** revealed that *the generation* that witnessed the 'fig tree' (Matthew 21:19>24:32, 33) sprouting again would not 'pass by' till all the things He signified throughout that latter chapter should occur.

Clearly the above scriptures are more literal than are generally recognised, as you have hopefully understood as a result of reading this publication.

Surely few would deny that we are living in a generation that is witnessing unprecedented numbers of 'battles and tidings of battles' ('wars and rumours of wars') [Matthew 24:6; Mark 13:7; Luke 21:9].

If in fact these (and many other) issues are clear indications that we are living in 'the last days', we need to recognize the validity of the scriptural warnings and act accordingly. Remember, the generation that survives the coming foretold events, which will intrude upon all mankind (Luke 21:34-36), will be keeping the Commandments of God and the teachings of Yaishua.

Is this the generation that **Yaishua** was referring to when He said, 'that by no means may this generation (which has increased by about *5½ billion* in this current generation to about 7½ billion and which is projected to reach a world-wide total of approximately *9½ billion* people by its end) be passing by till all these things should be occurring'?

It may be later than many currently realise—

My prayer is that the only true God, **YHWH**, will quicken the contents of this publication to whomever He wills and bless you in all ways and always, through His beloved Son **Yaishua** haMashiach.

The Greek Alphabet:

(8) THE UNCIAL AND CURSIVE GREEK ALPHABETS

Uncial			Cursive
Λ	ah	A	α
B	b	B	β
Γ	g	Γ	γ
Δ	d	Δ	δ
Є	e	E	ε
Z	dz	Z	ζ
H	ey	H	η
Θ	th	Θ	θ
I	ee	I	ι
K	k	K	κ
Λ	l	Λ	λ
M	m	M	μ
N	n	N	ν
Ξ	s	Ξ	ξ
O	o	O	ο
Π	p	Π	π
P	r	P	ρ
C	s	Σ	σ, ς
T	t	T	τ
Y	u	Y	υ
Φ	f	Φ	φ
X	ch	X	χ
Ψ	ps	Ψ	ψ
ω	o	Ω	ω

The letters of the Greek alphabet are easily learned. Indeed nearly half of them, A, B, E, I, K, M, N, O, T, Z, are precisely the same as in English in both force and form. C, though it is supposed to represent our S, has the same sound as soft C (as in cereal) or S. P is R. By observing oft-repeated forms they become familiar.

The uncial or primitive letters are shown at the left in their original forms, and faithfully reproduced, as far as possible, in these handmade replicas of the autograph copies.

The cursive or modern Greek characters are shown on the right.

CPSIA information can be obtained at www.ICGtesting.com
Printed in the USA
LVOW07s0737210115

423628LV00002B/14/P

9 781493 191949